Sermons by the Devil

Satanic Views and Advice

By William Shuler Harris

PANTIANOS
CLASSICS

Published by Pantianos Classics

ISBN-13: 978-1-78987-635-2

First published in 1904

Contents

Preface...vii

Introduction viii

Satan's Sermon on Suicide...9

Sermons on the River of Life... 13

A Serpent Sermon by Satan.. 18

Satan's Business Advice... 19

    A Reply to Satan's Business Advice 20

The Death of a Saloon-Keeper 21

A Sermon by Satan to a Dying Christian.. 25

Satan Preaches to a Society Woman 27

Preaching Behind Curtains... 28

Views of Satan on Lying.. 30

    Comments on the Foregoing Sermon 33

Little Sermons by Satan to Persuade People to Reject the Great
Invitation 33

Satan's Musical Sermon 40

Satan on Child Training... 41

    A Brief Reply to the Preceding Sermon on Training Children 43

Satan on Christian Zeal 43

    Comments on the Foregoing Sermon 44

Harmlessness of Sin – An Object Sermon by Satan....................... 45

    A Reply to Satan's Talk on the Harmlessness of Sin 45

The Lord's Supper.. 46

Family Worship 48

    A Reply to Satan on Family Worship 50

Satan and Purity 51

The Journey of Miss Pilgrim.. 55

A Time when Satan Failed 64

How to Conduct Revival Meetings.. 66

    A Reply to the Sermon by Satan on Revival Meetings.......................68

A Tobacco Sermon by Satan.. 69

    A Few Comments on the Tobacco Sermon..71

The Devil's Free Lunch Counter 73

How to Keep People from Going to Church 74

Satan on Sensuality 79

The Bondage of Sin... 80

The Saloon Devil and Uncle Sam... 85

Let Us Alone - A Peculiar Sermon by the Devil on Luke 4:34 87

    Comments on the Above Sermon..91

The Hobby Factory 92

    Some Notes on the Remarks Made by Satan on the Hobby Factory........94

Preaching at the Bridge 95

Where the Devil Need Not Preach..100

Till All Comes Right...101

Two Kinds of Riches..102

Satan on Atheism 103

    A Reply to Satan's Talk on Atheism...105

Heaven and Hell...107

    Some Things Omitted by Satan 108

Sermons on Preaching 109

A Reply to the Preceding Sermon 112

Sermons on Prayer, by Satan and Members of his Cabinet 113

Satan's Sermon on Jonah 117

Comments on the Preceding Pages 119

Satan's Views on Swearing 120

Seven Sermons by Members of the Devil's Cabinet 121

The Devil's Last Song 132

To my many friends who by their kindly criticisms pro and con have made it easier for me to write, and who have urged me to the completion of this volume, this book is sincerely dedicated.

Preface

The part that Satan plays in the drama of a human life is often larger than a person will admit. Each one of us is not only acting, but we are constantly acted upon by one or the other of two great influences. The Good Spirit endeavors to lead us to the skies, and its angels are ever willing to minister to our real needs. The Evil Spirit, either openly or under cover, seeks to destroy our mind with the untruth by preaching to us his black sermons of death. Some of these sermons are short, others are longer, and at times they are delivered to us in the language of an angel with all the dignity that good scholarship might command.

This volume was commenced with the purpose of tearing off his Satanic mask so that people might see more clearly the real source of these dark sermons. There are many people who, after yielding to temptation, will declare that they have acted independent of any evil influence. Satan is pleased to see a person rest in the shadow of such a delusion, but it is better for each one of us to know that either the good or evil spirit is seeking to be the guest of our thoughts, and it depends upon our attitude who will be entertained.

The most deceived man of all is he whose mind is influenced by the Evil Spirit and yet he believes that he is besought by the Good Spirit. We hope to reach some of such persons whose eyes are color blind and whose ears are so impaired that they alone cannot distinguish between the voices that are calling them downward and those that are calling them upward.

We aimed to keep the book clean throughout, even though we tried to bring out the real character of the unclean Spirit. *We have advanced only such arguments of Satan as he uses continually in his practical dealings with people.* We were particular that none of the chapters should be a source of temptation, but that they might give Satan his proper setting more clearly in the minds of the reader, and thereby destroy the edge of his sword as much as possible.

To the art work of this book the most careful attention has been given, both by the author and the famous artist, Paul Krafft, of New York. Neither work nor money was spared to produce the most accurate drawings so as to assist the mind in grasping the truths of the book. And now, that the volume is completed, it is the fond hope of the writer that it may not fall short of its purpose. The author sought the aid of Divine wisdom in producing this book, and he now depends upon the same power to carry it into the channels of His own choosing.

The Author.

May 12, 1904.

Introduction

In some instances when the author of a book is unknown it is customary to secure some noted person to write the Introduction. It is unnecessary, however, in the presentation of this book to the public, inasmuch as its able author is so well known. Those who have read his former works are numbered by the hundreds of thousands. When an author's writings have been received with such a welcome and endorsed with such a phenomenal sale, not only in his own country, but also in other lands, it is unnecessary to introduce him and his works, as his name is already in the hearts of the people.

We want to say that this book, entitled "Sermons by the Devil," is original and unique from cover to cover, and that the author spent much time and thought in its preparation. We believe that it is the crowning work of his life.

The illustrations have been drawn by the genius, Paul Krafft, and they are the best of his efforts. Each picture is a careful study and is perfected with much painstaking work. We have saved neither time nor expense to make this one of the best books ever put before the people for the low price we are asking for it.

We hope that this work will be received with welcome in millions of homes and that its good mission will not be misunderstood. The book will surely do much good, and any one helping to distribute it will be sowing seed that will bear a rich harvest long after his earthly life is ended. In these times of wickedness and greed there is great need of a spiritual awakening, and a book of this character is well calculated to reach the desired object. It is our hope that all this and even more will be accomplished through the influence of this book.

The Publishers.

Satan's Sermon on Suicide

Satan was making earnest efforts to persuade a certain man to commit suicide. He tempted him at midnight as far as the center of the bridge, and as the man hesitated to spring into the water, Satan continued speaking:

"I congratulate you as you stand here on the very edge of genuine happiness. If you have sufficient courage, you will soon enter into perfect peace. Look down upon the sweet waters, and see how they invite you to the most peaceful kind of a death. They promise to cover all your cares and troubles, and put you to sleep on the bosom of the deep."

A good angel interrupted these temptations of Satan:

"Spring not from this bridge, for such an act will bring no relief to your poor soul. It would be the opening of the door through which you would enter to experience deeper sorrows and grief more terrible. Listen no longer to the voice that points you toward the pangs of death."

The words of the angel touched the heart of the man and they seemed to draw him away, but Satan again quickly spoke:

"Don't be a coward. Have you not found that the best joys of this life are worthless, and that your troubles are so great that you can no longer bear them I Why be so foolish as to continue under this load, to live on in misery and wretchedness? You have gone thus far towards peace, and now one plunge from the bridge will end all your woes."

Again the angel insisted:

"Nay! nay! be not so foolhardy. Before you lies not only the dark waters, but the judgment bar of God. If you listen and heed the voice of Satan, you are responsible for the result of listening. You cannot plead any excuse for self-murder, inasmuch as God has sent me, as one of his angels, to warn you while the warmth of life is yet yours. Return to your tasks; face your situation; forsake sin and take God into your life, then your troubles will no longer seem unsurmountable. By God's help, you will be given the best solution of the problem that vexes you, and your life will yet be crowned with honor and glory. Let God drop life's curtain, but do not draw it yourself."

These kindly words had a great influence on the heart of this man. Once more he was about to turn and walk toward the city, but the enemy with bold audacity, again continued his sermon:

"What can you see ahead of you as you lift your eyes? Have you not tried the theatre, and what joy can that give? Have you not tried the ways of prostitution, and what lasting comfort have you found? Have you not tasted of the wine glass, and found no satisfying portion? In brief, is it not true that everything has failed to give you the peace for which you have been vainly sighing? You must not be deceived by false voices that call you to imaginary peace. Religion is a failure, and you need not think of depending upon the church or Sunday School for any real comfort. The world would be far better off if there were no churches. The only work they do is to annoy the consciences of people while they live, and in many instances, cast a heavy gloom over them in death." The Devil paused just a moment and then in a softer voice continued: "Since all of your prospects are like bubbles, why not leap instantly into the waters, whose velvety touches shall smooth down all your cares and bury you in peace forever! There is no grave like that of the water. Look now upon its smiling face and remember that all those silent moonlight beckonings are inviting you to the deepest and most sublime comfort. Hesitate no more. Why not carry your whole purpose to a finish? There could be nothing sweeter than to fall from this bridge. The rest will all follow like the evening follows noon, or like the bright stars follow the heat of a closing day."

At this the man actually leaned over and was looking thoughtfully into the waters below him. Then the good angel lovingly entreated him once more:

"Think of your mother and your friends. Look at the disgrace you will leave behind you. Remember, God, who made the waters, made them not to comfort a dying man. There is no peace to be found in such a manner of ending life. Empty your mind of these vain delusions which I assure you are but temptations from the Devil. If you heed his voice you will find, when it is too late, that you will be in the power of the very wretch who now seeks your ruin."

Then did the Devil whisper a few long sentences so low that no one could hear but the listener. It was a terrible temptation playing upon the man in his weakness. It was his purpose to heed the voice of the good angel, but he somehow felt that he was being drawn away from the light that was trying to enter his soul, and so, in the desperation that was born of this thought, he seized his enemy as if in bodily conflict, and taking advantage of the advice previously given to him by the angel, he called upon God for help. After a sharp decisive struggle Satan was pushed off of the bridge, but it seemed as if he did not fall into the water. The man quickly turned for he felt a saving hand upon him, and to his happiness he found that the angel had not let go of him during all the conflict. Never did any creature seem so beautiful as the angel appeared to him at that moment. He had conquered in the conflict, and next he breathed out his petition on the midnight air that God might help him through the troubles that had almost overwhelmed him. His prayer was answered and over the wrecks of a wasted life he reared a building of character and wealth that he humbly dedicated to the unseen God.

It is sad to relate that not all of the sons and daughters of the human race conquer Satan when they are subjected to the terrible temptations of self destruction.

Every inward voice or suggestion that urges a man to self-destruction is born of Satan. Look at the picture and see how the Black Demon points downward. He is urging the man to find comfort in suicide. That is the best recipe that Satan and infidelity can offer to a person who is overwhelmed with trouble. Let such a one turn a deaf ear to Satan's temptation and listen to the Angel of Light who will point him to the Son of Righteousness by day and the Star of Hope by night.

Then the Devil whispered a few long sentences, urging the man to commit suicide, and the good angel once more endeavored to draw the man away.

On the great river of life Satan will steer free of charge any boat that drifts downward. They who work upward toward heaven and success will be crowned both here and hereafter.

Sermons on the River of Life

The river of life rises at the gate of Heaven and empties into the ocean of Death. At the age of accountability each individual is launched into the stream about midway, and he must either drift with the current downward or work against it upward. The river flows with different degrees of rapidity as you go from the shore toward its center. The chief end of human life is for one to struggle against the natural currents and push his way farther and farther up the stream toward Heaven and Success.

It is very easy to move with the current. Idleness is a drifting toward death. There are many things along the banks of this river to attract attention, so that by looking intently toward the shore, no one will realize that he is surely drifting toward the black waters of Destruction. It is the purpose of Satan to engage one's thought in any manner whatever so as to keep his hands from plying the oars against the stream.

Happy the person who refuses to give his time and his thought to the light-some attractions along the way, or to the inward temptations that are direct-ly prompted by Satan. It must be remembered that if anything good is to be obtained in this life, one cannot get it without an effort. There are plenty of good things up the river. The farther you travel upward, the more beautiful are the flowers along the banks, and the more wholesome fruits can be plucked from the branches overhanging the stream. Also in those higher places, there are cool and shady inlets where one may rest in peace on the pure waters, in the beauty of the fresh and balmy air.

But strange to say, there are comparatively few who are willing to make a sacrifice in order to reach these happy places farther up the stream. Some pride themselves by saying that they are as good as certain other people, but it happens that those other people are slowly drifting down stream. One should not find satisfaction in making the same progress that somebody else is making who is drifting down toward the ocean of Death.

Far down this stream, the waters become dark and filthy and the climate is sickening, but they who are drifting past the lowlands become accustomed to the climate and really do not seem to know that they are moving in such an unwholesome atmosphere.

In the light of these truths, one can readily see how easy it is to sin, even though its consequences are hard to bear. Sinning need be nothing more than drifting down stream into the poisoned atmosphere where all kinds of impurities exist. The end of such a course is spiritual death and all of its at-tached penalties.

It is possible to obtain good things in our natural life by inheritance or in some other way that costs us no labor, but on the mighty river of life you must not think that you can go up stream by luck. It is your duty to pull the oars against the current, and if your arms are weak, you will get all needed strength. "Man's extremity is God's opportunity." If you have a poor boat or a poor pair of oars, Heaven asks no more of you than the best you can do, after which, strange to say, your cumbersome bark will make remarkable progress up stream.

It may be true that some will pass you even up the stream, but do not become faint-hearted. Not always those who travel with rapid spurts make the most progress in the end. Some who bend their energies with all diligence for a season, are suddenly attracted and give their attention to some object of peculiar interest, and lo, their boat goes drifting again down stream.

The humble, faithful worker in his effort to travel up stream will naturally meet with many oppositions, but if he is persistent and surrender to no temptation, he will surely come to the place where rowing is less difficult and where the immediate banks will give him better subjects for reflection. By and by he will be called from the stream of life to take up his residence in the Celestial City.

As you study the condition of life on this wonderful river it is hard to believe that there could be anybody whose main object would be to urge people to travel down stream. This is the work that Satan is doing with all his power. He is constantly advancing false arguments to persuade all classes of people to take life easy as far as spiritual matters are concerned. The companies who are traveling down stream will aggregate into the millions.

It is a common sight to see the Devil flattering a young man who finds that the natural current is too slow for him. Satan tells such a man to ply his oars down stream, and one is horrified to see with what rapidity the young man is rushing ahead toward his destruction. In his madness he acts as if he wishes to see the whole program of sin as soon as possible. What does he care for warning voices? He sings a jolly song and shuts his ears to every loving cry as he feasts his sensual eyes upon the moral impurities along the way. The Devil laughs at him while others weep.

And then perchance, as he dashes ahead in his reckless course, his hooked boat will take hold of another and drag its occupant on towards the same destruction. If his comrade is not willing to take his same pace down stream, he will either urge him against his will, or will cast him off as one who is tied to his mother's apron strings. Such a reckless youth will always find women who will equal him in his terrible career downward. Amongst this blind class of people there are not a few who become so hardened in sin that they deliberately throw their oars away, thus throwing away their best chance of traveling against the current. Such a person is just as foolish as a bird who would cut off its wings because it felt tired after taking a long flight.

I saw one young man in his extremity who not only threw away his oars, but pounded at the very bottom of his boat until it sprang a leak so that he was drawn down to a watery grave.

I saw on this same river of life another boat carrying a few pleasure seekers. Those on board had their minds so wrapt up in the enjoyments of this life that they paid no attention to the more serious duties of reaching success. Satan gladly improved the opportunity of occupying a seat on this same boat and steering it. He knew just where to steer the boat so that they would be farther away from the missionary voices that were ever calling in order to save souls from a downward life of sin. There was a Hellish smile that played upon the face of the grim monster as he noticed the thoughtlessness and frivolity of those on board. Satan offers to steer any craft free of charge, but the price is often so great that one becomes bankrupt when he tries to settle the bill. The deception of Satan is unspeakable and he is mean enough to get others to point the finger of scorn at a person who may be struggling hard against the current in order to reach Heaven and success.

I was indeed glad that I was privileged to see on this same river one of the nobler characters who occupied a humble boat. He was striving with all reasonable effort to push his boat upstream, and in this noble work he was opposed by the imps of Hell and by a number of companions who called him foolish for not taking in the sights farther down the stream. His purpose was fixed, and no one could swerve him from his course even though a score or more tried to shipwreck the young man. His heart was thrilled with joy because he was in touch with the wish of the infinite mind. And more than that there was an angel who was sent to crown him with one of those kind of crowns that all good people get before they reach Heaven. One is not compelled to wait until he reaches the gate of Heaven before his joy begins. As mentioned before, there are unspeakable pleasures along the stream of life to those who continue ever upward, and the angels are always interested in the progress such a one is making.

The names of the two oars are Faith and Works. If these are both worked together, effective work can be done. No one can make any progress up stream if he fails to use either one of these oars. There are quite a few pilgrims who are led to think that faith is of more consequence than works and others who believe that works is more important than faith. Such people make very blundering progress by working one oar more than the other. They go swinging around in circles and strike against shore at the wrong places. Thus in this roundabout manner the chances are that the current will somewhat carry them downward, to say nothing of the spectacle they present to those who are looking on.

I heard the Devil preaching a little sermon to an earnest Christian whose mind was biased toward faith. He told the Christian that faith was everything, and that works count for nothing as far as spiritual progress is concerned. "It all depends upon what a man believes and not so much what he does, whether he will ever reach Heaven." That does not mean that a man can commit evil deeds with impunity and not suffer for it, but it simply teaches that the heart must be right in its belief and that that alone will count for righteousness. If you would be a power in the world let me urge you to accept and teach this doctrine most gladly, so that others who are in the dark, and who are constantly worrying about their works may be brought into the full light.

The very same day that I heard the Devil preaching this little sermon on the great importance of faith, I heard him preach another little sermon in which he put works on top. He was speaking to a good woman who was making fair progress against the current. In some way he attracted her attention long enough to plant his evil thoughts into her mind.

"My dear Christian friend," he urged, "it is almost impossible for a person to know what is the true nature of faith, and this being true, I would urge you to cease worrying over this subject, and see to it that you do good works. If you give proper attention to the latter, then happiness and progress will smile upon you more than ever. After all the most important thing in life is good works. Follow this advice and be happy."

The woman who always had some difficulty in understanding faith was very glad to hear this doctrine again brought to her attention even though she had often heard it before. She was anxious to follow this new advice and consequently she commenced to work the oar called Works. You well know what happened, and as the boat swung in a circle she made herself believe that this was an improved way of making progress. She tried to exercise pity toward those who were wise enough to make use of both oars. It then occurred to my mind that the worst conceit in the world is that which makes a person believe that his religious ideas are better than those of any other people who are trying to do right.

It would be a long story if we were to tell the principal happenings on this famous river. Your heart would be filled with rapturous delight if we were to describe the manner in which the travelers are received after they have reached the end of their upward journey. Heaven and Success are awaiting many more who are pushing up stream. This is the bright part of the whole scene.

But it would be impossible for us to describe the extremely horrible condition of things as you go to the lower end of the stream, neither could we relate the untold horrors of the ocean of spiritual death which is a receptacle of all the filth and slime of sin and sinners.

Each human being is somewhere on this river, either drifting downward toward the one extreme or rowing upward toward the gates of the Eternal City. Such a tiling as remaining stationary on this river is unthinkable, although many who imagine that they are continuing about the same, do not realize that they are actually floating downward.

Small sins grow like small serpents, and if not conquered, will take their victims down to death.

A Serpent Sermon by Satan

Preached along the pathway of life to those who give heed.

Along the pathway of life there are scattered a large number of beautiful buildings with costly furnishings. These are supplied with little pet snakes of sin, which can be had, free of charge, by all who are willing to accept them.

Certain snakes are kept on exhibition, and as they lie in their beautiful glass cases, they present a handsome appearance. They have neat ribbon bows tied around their necks, and certain sides of the boxes are lined with satin. In front of one of these buildings I heard a man calling out:

"Come this way! come this way! all ye who hear my voice. We have on exhibition some beautiful bosom pets. If you take one now, while it is young and small, you can train it to your liking, and I will assure you that you will not only have a novel pet, but that you will be safe from its poison forever."

A certain young man, who was passing near by, was attracted to the place, and with suspicion, he glanced at the curious little pets.

"Are these not deadly snakes that you offer?"

"Ha! ha!" laughed the Evil One, "that is what some people call them, but I assure you that you need not fear them. If you take to your bosom one of these beautiful so-called deadly pets, you will not only be free from danger but it will give new warmth to your heart as you hold it there."

"I don't like the appearance of the pets," commented the young man.

"Perhaps the appearance of some may shock you a little at first, but if you will look over the whole assortment, you will find one that will suit your fancy altogether."

Then the wicked fiend spoke very fluently about the effect that these little charmers had on the present life. His words were making a favorable impression on the young man, who considered himself proof against all forms of temptation. Strange to say, the very snake that had impressed him so horribly a short time before, now fascinated him altogether. He stood as if charmed by the little serpent that the black agent held coiled in his hand.

"This is my choice," said the young man who willingly agreed to pay the price, which was nothing more than his promise to give it a place above his heart.

The young man carried the little serpent in his breast and allowed it to feed upon his heart's blood. The snake grew so slowly that the owner did not realize with what increasing danger it was sapping his life's energies. He was unconsciously nursing an enemy, and thereby inviting his own ruin and death. The serpent had now grown large enough that it could playfully wrap itself around the arm or waist of the young man.

In the course of time the foolish young man saw very clearly that if he would not conquer the serpent that the serpent would conquer him. So he resolved to shake the serpent off or kill it in the attempt. He never realized until then how it had fastened itself upon his very vitals, and that he was powerless in his own strength to overcome the enemy. A long and terrible battle was fought. The serpent swung itself mightily in the great battle and the young man, in desperation, seized it and tried to crush it with his hands or stamp it with his feet. The serpent was more than a match for the youth, who called out mightily for help, and in response to his pleadings a good angel came to him and said:

"Let Christ into your heart and he will destroy the deadly serpent of sin and will make you free again."

To these welcome words the young man gave heed and was almost persuaded to accept Christ when Satan, robed like an angel, stole to his side and whispered:

"Don't be foolish, young man. You must not expect to find help from some outside power, you are fully able to help yourself. Since you are blessed with a strong mind of your own, why go begging like a little child for help? Is it not more honorable to die like a hero fighting your own battle, than to be a weakling or a coward?"

"But I will be forever lost, if I don't get rid of this sin. I cannot conquer it myself, for I have already spent all my energy in trying to do so."

Then Satan tempted him another way by appealing to his pride, and after that by trying to frighten him. But all these proved futile, and the young man turned to the better angel and to Christ who is able to deliver. His repentance and confession brought down the power that destroyed the serpent, and the young man rejoiced greatly in his freedom.

Satan's Business Advice

"If a man enter upon some kind of business to gain a livelihood for himself and family, it is his duty to so conduct his affairs as to make it pay.

A business man has the right to perform certain tricks which in themselves are perfectly proper, even though the world or the church may condemn them. People who are not in business do not fully understand how many intricate problems there are to solve and how many little trials there are to bear."

"To state the whole matter briefly, I would say that a soft, tender conscience and a wide-awake business man make poor companions. If you wish to succeed in business you must observe the following rules:

1. "Learn to prevaricate without lying."

"Prevarication is pleasing to the people and without it you will have a disappointed class of customers. It is certain that people expect you to shade the truth a little, or they would not ask such foolish questions most every time they come to purchase. If you are selling an article worth one dollar, the customer is pleased if you tell him that it is worth two dollars. He is not particular whether you are telling the truth or not. All he cares about is that he can tell his friends that he is wearing an article worth two dollars."

2. "Become expert in the use of 'bluff.'"

"Bluff is the most modern way of lying without violating the law. In purchasing goods you can so talk that the manufacturer will believe that you can buy cheaper elsewhere. If you put these bluffs at him in a modern style, it may compel him to yield, and perchance you may clear several dollars in your deal."

3. "You must learn to make heavy profits wherever you can."

"Your policy should be to get for an article what you can and not what is right. You will find that before you are through with your business career that you need all the margins that it is possible for you to make. You should, as quickly as possible, have a reserve fund so as to be prepared for any emergency."

4. "You must learn the art of adulteration and make use of this knowledge to best advantage."

5. "In order to avoid competition, form a monopoly if possible."

"This is the great secret of large business success. You could not expect to become a power in the business world so long as you are hampered with a lot of small trade centers, each one doing a business similar to your own. The motto of the age is: Combine interests, either drown out or buy out the small firms, and get a full control of the line of business which you represent. Do not allow the cries of a weak reformer or a nervous public to make you believe that this is wrong. You must stick to the policy that anything is right that you can do and escape from the civil law."

A Reply to Satan's Business Advice

When one studies the methods of Satan in the business world he is strongly impressed with the numberless ways in which dishonesty and deception are practiced under a cloak of righteousness. Satan says with a show of boldness that "A tender conscience and a wide-awake business man make poor companions." This is a false statement and is only believed by the man or woman whose conscience has already been warped. In business or in any other vocation the only way to reach real success is by the way of honesty. It is true that a rascal may endure for a season, and heap unto himself great wealth and thus appear to enjoy the highest success in life, but all this will prove in the end a curse to him.

The majority of those who fail in business are not the conscientious men, but those who have had their ears open, more or less, to Satan's business advice. We have a sure word of prophecy that rings out the following note: "As the partridge sitteth on her eggs, and hatcheth them not; so he that getteth riches, and not by right, shall leave them in the midst of his days, and at his end shall be a fool." Jer. 17-11.

Satan gives a few rules which he claims must be observed if one would wish to reach success in business. The first one is "Learn to prevaricate with-

20

out lying." This is only another way of saying, learn to tell a falsehood without lying. The only safe way in business is to tell the truth. By doing so, you may occasionally lose a sale or a customer but your loss will be your gain. Your truthful qualities will lift you gradually to a substantial throne of honor.

"Bluff" is the refuge of the hypocrite. There are times when one has a right to pass off a pleasantry or an innocent joke, but whenever anything of this kind is used to cover real facts in a business deal, then it changes to the color of a lie.

In the third advice given by Satan there is a peculiar mingling of truth and error and it is in such kinds of arguments that Satan ripens the mind for greater error. It is not always right to get what you can for a commodity. There is a difference between might and right and there are thousands who take advantage of situations especially in monopolizing, and by getting what they can they get considerably more than what is right or just. There is no rule in business so precious as the Golden Rule.

One need not resort to unlawful adulteration or to any other type of illegal or unrighteous actions. This is the Devil's pathway of success down to eternal destruction. If you are honest and righteous to your full ability, you will enjoy the peace of a clear conscience through all your business years, and in the evening of life you will have precious meditations and the sweetest reflections. And most glorious of all when your eyes close to this life, Eternity will dawn with a full radiance of immortal glory and you will be receiving your reward forever.

The Death of a Saloon-Keeper

NOTE: The following incident is taken from actual life. It is no imaginary sketch or fanciful picture. The author is not sure whether it was a case of delirium tremens or not.

Satan appeared to a saloon-keeper who was lying in great stress upon his deathbed, and spoke to him as follows:

"Let me give you one more sermon, old fellow, before you reach your reward. You have done a noble service. You have served me well, and surely I will not forsake you in this hour of death. You need not become frightened at my presence. Come! come! stop your agitations," continued the Devil, "you need not be alarmed."

"Oh horrors! oh horrors!" shrieked the poor man, "would to God that I could have a new lease of life! How can I go out into this darkness alone?"

"I will be with you to hold your hand, and lead you to your reward," assured the Devil.

Then the poor wretch tried to concentrate his thoughts on noble things, but his sins arose before him like mountains, and he could review their terrors before his eyes.

"The saloon-keeper shrank back upon his pillow and lifted his bony fingers in terror. X X X Satan and his imps continue to advance, and they all tried to look as beautiful as possible."

"O! what shall I do with my sins; my awful sins; my many, many sins?" he groaned aloud.

"Trouble yourself not, forget about them and be at peace," came the voice of Satan, whose real form was now gradually unfolding itself to the dying man, at which the saloon-keeper shrank back upon his pillow and lifted his bony fingers in terror.

"Keep back! keep back! come no nearer," continued his heart-breaking appeals. Satan and his imps continued to advance and they all tried to look as beautiful as possible. But they could no longer mask themselves. The struggling man tried to find rest by fastening his eyes elsewhere. But the terrible visage of Satan was so appalling, that he could not take his eyes therefrom.

Death drew still nearer and the struggle of the unfortunate man became more intense. He made one last effort to seek refuge somewhere, but just at that moment, each one of the little company of imps presented his claim. This so distracted the mind of the man that his actions were similar to a raving maniac.

"I claim your love," demanded the first imp.

"And I claim your time," demanded another, whose grinning countenance was most terrible to behold.

"I demand your attention," spoke a third in a tone most grinding and severe.

"I demand your talents throughout all eternity," spoke the most horrible imp of all the company.

"And I demand your sacrifices to be given willingly in the kingdom to come," cried out another.

And still another in mockery said: "I demand your service," but before the imp had finished his words, Satan himself cried out, "I demand your soul, your life, your all." At this saying the imps formed a cordon around the bed, and the miserable man crouched anew at their uncanny movements.

He had been sick for many weeks and refused nearly all food. He had so fallen away in flesh that scarcely anything but skin lay over his bones. His eyes were sunken and he presented an awful appearance as he was struggling in a terrible effort to escape from the cordon of imps.

He sprang back against the head-board of the bed, lifting his bony fingers like claws, as he screamed out: "Take them away! take them away!" His cries were so horrible that no one could remain in the room with him, even his wife was compelled to leave and not one of his old chums could stand so terrible a picture of death. Some one hastened to the home of a minister in the midnight hour, and urged him to come up at once to the hotel, and pray with the dying man. The minister hastily dressed and with Bible in hand, soon entered the hotel and noticed the terror-stricken people all around, who begged him to go into the next room and do what he could for the poor man. The situation tested the courage of the minister, for as he approached the room, he heard the unearthly shrieks of the dying man, and upon opening the door, found that all had deserted the room. He prayed for courage, and thus

"The sweet angels carried him in abounding triumph above the enemy's reach. Where his liberated soul could hear the music ok the spheres and the choirs invisible."

strengthened he walked with a steady tread up to the bedside of the man, and opened his Bible before him. Suddenly there was a calm, and for the first time in many hours, the poor wretch sank down upon his pillow in quietness.

At this sudden turn, some ventured into the room and all stood as still as death, and the dying man lay motionless, as the minister read from the word of God and spoke to him. It seemed that even the devils dared not advance farther while the Word of God was being uttered in their hearing.

The minister, after a long conference, found that nothing more could be done and was compelled to go. After he had left the room, the same terrible scenes followed. The poor wretch continuously cried out in anguish and in the pathos of appealing: "Take them away! keep them back!" No one could check the march of the very devils that were advancing to claim their own, and not being able to remain in the room they all forsook him again.

All this terrible tragedy continued until the poor body of the dying man left go of its spirit, which seemed to satisfy this pack of demons, like a piece of flesh quiets a pack of pursuing wolves.

If a person is prepared to meet death he can pass out of this life in mighty triumph, but what can be more terrible than the death of the wicked? To such death comes in its worst features. Some may not die with shrieks of terror on their lips, but their inward pangs cannot be described. The picture on the opposite page does not exaggerate the horrible experiences of some who have rejected God through life. The Evil Spirits can be seen best when the curtain of mortality is falling. The only way to a happy death is by a righteous life.

A Sermon by Satan to a Dying Christian

Satan knows that it pays to preach a sermon to one. He clings to the proverb: "Handpicked fruit is the choicest." He crowded his way to the side of a dying man, and tried to interject his deathly sentences.

"At last the long-looked-for event is at hand. You are now entering the dark shadows of death, and will find that your Christian faith is worthless in this hour of your greatest need. Religion may be good enough to live by, but it is a poor staff upon which to lean at such a time as this. Death and religion can no more mix than oil and water. The imaginary power of Christ to save you, may be a comfort to you in the ordinary days of life, but in the presence of so stem a reality as death, it is of no avail. Therefore you have prayed and served in vain, and I urge you to forsake God as you feel the effects of this terrible darkness creeping upon you."

"Paul may have cried out, 'O death, where is thy sting.' Any man could talk that way when he was so far away from death as Paul was. Let me assure you that there is a sting to death, so sharp that no one can evade its pangs. The richest of all the earth, with the poorest, have alike shared its stings. If the graves could open their mouths, they would speak dark words to you more convincing than any of the arguments that I could put forth."

Then the dying man, feeling the dark breath of temptation upon him, shouted out in clear words: "Stand back, ye demons of darkness. Make room for the coming King and his angels." But Satan refused to move an inch. He stood defiantly and with a show of boldness spake again:

"I have a claim upon you, and you must not think that you can push me away so lightly. What care I for a convoy of angels or your so-called Master. All such nonsense is only an outgrowth of your diseased imagination. Listen to me and stop this wild dreaming and these foolish actions. Why stand on such a flimsy foundation when you are in need of a rock? Once more I urge you to forsake your God, your Christ, your Bible and your experience, and I will reward you a thousand times more by and by."

Then, from one unseen, came the words softly but in tones of deep assurance:

"Yea, though I walk through the valley of the shadow of death, I will fear no evil, for thou art with me, they rod and thy staff they comfort me."

The dying man was strengthened by these sweet sentences, and without fear he commanded the tempter: "Away from me, you deceiver, I will triumph through the blood of the Lamb and in the name of Him who holds the keys of Death and Hell."

"I will not away until my claim is settled," stoutly declared the enemy.

"Again I say stand back. You are a Devil, a robber, a liar, full of all subtlety. If you will not go at my words, I now command you to leave me in the name of Jesus Christ my Redeemer."

At this Satan drew his foul length to one side only to make room for a hideous monster called Death, who by its awful presence, hoped to attract the attention of the dying man from his faith.

"What terrible creature is this?" gasped the dying man in his weakening breath.

"This is death itself," answered Satan in threatening tones, "and be assured that nothing like the faith of religion can overcome its presence. I command you once more to forsake your religion and your God and trust yourself to me."

Then did the dying man lift his eyes of faith steadfastly above, just as death would have sent its sharp sting into his soul. Happy was the man to find that he was covered with a shield that not only kept away the stings, but also hid the form of the terrible monster. Then came a flood of light from the celestial world, which revealed to him a new vision of his blessed Redeemer who had conquered Death, Hell and the Grave.

This same Redeemer with his outstretched hand touched the dying saint upon the head, and filled him with glory unspeakable. As the Christian breathed his last breath, he felt a dull thud of the enemy's attack, but it struck no more than the shield behind which he was safe forever. Christ caught him away from the darksome shadows, and the sweet angels carried him in abounding triumph above the enemy's reach where his liberated soul could hear the music of the spheres and the choirs invisible.

Satan Preaches to a Society Woman

Subject: The disgrace of having children.

"What a blessed creature you are that fortune has smiled upon you so graciously. In the possession of so much wealth you have the noblest thing in life, for it is the means whereby everything else can be secured, and is indeed the secret of all true happiness. Money is power, and the absence of it causes dependence, misery and a long list of humiliating conditions."

"But of what use is your wealth if you do not allow it to bring you the greatest amount of happiness? If you would be true to society, and most sensible to yourself, you will see to it that in all your married life you will not be cursed with children. Let others, who are less fortunate than you, bear such burdens. You need all your time to fulfill your engagements, which are more numerous and more important by reason of your wealth. Disregard all this foolish talk about the inevitable yearning for motherhood, and hold your grand receptions and take your seasonable excursions and be ready at all times to enjoy the high and medium art of the stage."

"Why should your diamonds and your silks be idle for many months just for the purpose of having a child of your own, especially in these days when beautiful poodle dogs can be had for a mere song. Such creatures will not compel you to remain at home when you have a desire to go anywhere."

"If, in the hour of your weakness, you should crave for a cooing smile from a child of your own, or should wish, to enjoy the thrill of two baby eyes looking into your own, you must remember that these are blind calls of nature to which your sensitive heart need not give heed. You must learn as early in life as possible to be your own mistress and let judgment instead of sentiment control you."

"You can comfort yourself with the thought that the God of earth and Heaven has destined you to fill one of the noblest places in the society of earth. The real truth of the whole matter is this: the bearing of children is an eternal disgrace, but in order to comfort the women who impose upon themselves this condition, the poets and philosophers have lauded the mother with her children. Surely you need not share in the disgrace since you are enlightened, and since you have abundant wealth to keep you employed profitably all the time."

Some Things Satan Forgot To Put Into This Sermon

1. He forgot to tell this woman that the history of all ages proves that the disgrace rests upon the one in wedlock who refuses motherhood.

2. He forgot to tell her that if she heeded his doctrine her life would drift into an emptiness which nothing in the world could fill.

3. He also forgot to mention that all her wealth could not satisfy the instincts of human nature. The mother and the babe form a perfect pair, and each one needs the other to reach the highest happiness.

Preaching Behind Curtains

At last the Devil has succeeded in establishing certain churches, wherein his up-to-date business methods are employed. He claims that the church that offers religion at the lowest prices, and throws out the best inducements otherwise, will be patronized the most. Some churches agree to let people have religion for $10 a year, more or less. In these kinds of churches a person can do as he pleases, providing he is a little discreet about it. The Devil does not always advise a man to push his sin into daylight. He rather tells him to keep in the dark, and to be careful and pay his instalments to the church regularly.

As you look into some of the worldly churches and see what splendid offers they are making, you are not surprised that Satan is getting a foothold to an alarming extent. Wherever he is allowed, he stands behind the curtains, giving his inspiration and advice to all who will give heed. True enough there is a competition in church enterprises that is born of Heaven, but also, without a doubt, there is a rivalry that is prompted by the Devil.

The outgrowth of this unholy rivalry is seen far and wide. Much energy is expended so that one church may have more prestige than another. To accomplish this end, the church is guilty of countless follies and indiscretions, all practiced in the name of religion. Under such conditions Satan has more than little reason to rejoice.

Among the church organizations above referred to, the competition is somewhat after the fashion of business houses along the streets of a city. If your mind is unbiased and your eyes sharp enough, you can read many of the signs that these churches fling to the breeze. They are written in a beautiful and unassuming manner, but after they are faithfully interpreted into common English, some of them read as follows:

Repentance Very Cheap.
We Will Give You the Latest Kind;
Better Than Any. Other Church Offers
Apply at the Parsonage

Faith at Half-Price To-day.
A Few Remnants of the Old Style Left
Which We Offer Free,
As We Wish to Make Room for
The New Styles Just Imported.

We Have the Finest Church.
You Will Be
Just in it
If You Unite With Us.

Confession of Christ.
We Can Point Out to You
Some New and Easy Ways
of Satisfying
The Demands of Christ
Without Humiliation to Yourself.

Religion on Easy Terms.
The Whole Consignment Delivered at Once,
To be Paid for
By Monthly Instalments.
No Other Church Offers an Equal Bargain,

We Have the Widest Doors.
You Can Easily Enter Our Church
With the World Under One Arm
and Christ Under the Other,

We Are Most Liberal on Baptism.
With or Without Water Will Do.
Walking Through the Rain Will Answer.

As a person sees the inducements offered by the church, he begins to understand why some churches are doing so little thorough work for the Master. Some churches by their actions, seem to advertise thus:

We Have the Finest Pews,
Cushioned Seats,
Easy Backs and
Comfortable in Every Way.

We Have a Swell Preacher,
One Who Observes the Styles.
His Education is "Out of Sight,"
His Manner is Graceful.
There is No Other Like Him.

Our Choir is the Finest in the City;
The Soprano is a Star,
The Alto Sings Like an Angel,
The Organist is an Expert Manipulator

The Devil has succeeded in getting some seemingly good people to advertise their own goodness somewhat after the following manner:

We Are Holy.
Better Than Other People.
What We Do is Right.
If You Don't Do As We Do,
Then You Are Wrong.

I Wear Plain Clothing —
Much Plainer Than You Wear.
My Clothing is Pleasing to God.
If Your Clothing
Is Not Like My Clothing
Then You Had Better Make
a Change.

I Understand the Bible Very Well —
Better Than You Do.
If Your Opinions Are Different
From Mine,
Then You Are Wrong.

Views of Satan on Lying

Expressed to a Church-Member who wished to know if a lie was ever justifiable.

"To tell the truth on the subject of lying is harder to do than some people imagine, just because certain persons believe a lie should not be told under any circumstances. If this last view were correct, then we would have an easy solution of a difficult problem. But when one is anxious to give the whole truth on this subject, he will look at it from a sensible standpoint, notwithstanding how much labor of thought must thereby be expended."

"There are certain times in life when it is right to tell a lie. I will therefore satisfy your wishes by giving a few instances when a lie is justifiable."

1. "When a lie is a harmless one."

"There are many times when you can tell a lie that will do a great amount of good and will do no harm to the one you tell it. Anybody ought to know that under such circumstances it would not be wrong to lie. If we had more lying of this kind there would be more people made happy. How foolish a person is to think that he must tell the truth even when it results in a great amount of suffering, envy or disgrace. Of course, if the lie is calculated to do an injury to your neighbor, then that gives a new color to the whole situation, and you should hesitate at such a time."

2. "You have a right to tell a lie if you aim thereby to do good to the church or somebody else."

"To speak the truth at all times will only mean that you will be in trouble over half the time. But to tell a lie so that good may be done by it will keep things running smoothly and peace will prevail. In telling a lie be sure to cover your tracks as you go so that your lie will be hidden. If your falsehood should be discovered it will tend to weaken your influence with those whom you know. Remember it is not the lying that hurts a person, it is only when the lie is found out. My advice to you is to go ahead and make all the plans you can for the furthering of anything good in the church or outside of the church, and when you find that you cannot carry out your plans in an easy natural way of truth, then manufacture some lie by which you can push your scheme through. In this way you can do a great amount of good, and you must give the lie the credit for helping you to success. I think you will have no difficulty in seeing this point, and hope you will experience no trouble in following this advice."

3. "It is certainly proper to tell a lie if you wish to save somebody from a shock or spare him from mental anxiety or pain."

"You will be surprised to know how many people there are who are so squeezed up in a straight jacket that their consciences trouble them if they tell a lie even as an act of mercy. I met a man a short time ago who was sent to break the news to a poor mother that her husband was killed. When he first reached her, he spoke of her husband as being taken ill very suddenly and that he would be brought home. After the poor woman was nerved to this sad report, he told her still further that he feared that he would not be alive until he would reach home. Thus by gradual steps he prepared her mind for the arrival of her dead companion. After the man had done his work and returned to his home, his conscience upbraided him because he had at first misrepresented the situation to the widow."

"I will let you form your own conclusion concerning this case. Now if it is right to cover up the truth in such an instance, is it not also right to tell a lie under similar circumstances? Suppose a church-member hears a damaging rumor against herself which is being circulated over the whole community. I would consider it the act of an angel if somebody would tell her that the rumor is without any foundation whatever, and that it was never started as it is now being circulated. Suppose a husband has been unfaithful to his wife, would it not be perfectly proper for some one to tell a lie by saying that she was laboring under a misapprehension? Would it not be a great comfort to her if you could make her believe that she was wrong in her suspicions? So I could go on and give you many instances in which it would be proper to tell a lie. Let me once more urge an important point. Be sure, when you tell a lie, that you are reasonably safe from being detected."

4. "It is proper to tell a lie when you hope to be charitable to somebody. The Bible is so full of teaching on charity that you will be glad for an opportunity to practice it in this manner."

"If a person has a fault, and some one asks you about that person, would it not be kind in you to cover up the fault? If a person has an ugly disposition, would it not be kindness on your part to conceal this characteristic? Suppose a person is cursed with a bad temper, would it not be an act of charity if you were to speak kindly of his weakness to some one else? Always make some kind of an apology for the sins and weaknesses of others, so that the burdens of the weak will be lightened. As you walk along the pathway of life, you will find many opportunities of this kind to improve. How could you fulfill scripture more than if you practice after this advice. This kind of charity you can practice, and how can you do it without the convenient use of a little falsehood now and then."

5. "You certainly have a right to tell a lie to a person who asks you about things that he should not know, or about something that is not his business to know."

"What better treatment can you give a man with such a nose, than to grease it with the oil of deception? The more lies you can tell such a man the quicker he will awake and see that he is a fool. About the worst thing you can give to a nosy man is your valuable time. If you wish to tell such men everything they want to know, you can let your business drop and take care of such fellows the rest of your days. A good lie fitly spoken is like a cool breeze on a hot day. If you become expert in the use of lies you can deliver them evenly balanced. A lie will help you out of many a tight place and will put happiness right in your pathway many a time when otherwise you would find thorns to prick you."

"There are many other instances in which a lie is justifiable but I must leave all this to your own good judgment. I will give you a safe rule which you can follow: 'Whenever you feel like telling a lie and your conscience does not smite you, then you can feel sure that a lie is in place and you need not hesitate to tell it. If you should get into trouble sometime by telling a falsehood, you must not be too quick to blame all your trouble on the falsehood. You must remember that if you had not told the lie, that you might have gotten into greater trouble. That is the real oil of comfort which you must pour upon your wounded heart, when you are sorrowing over the lies which you have told.'"

"I wish you abundant success in life, and do not forget that by telling the truth at the right time and a lie at the right time, that you will learn the real secret of a successful career, either in the professions, in business, or in any one of the other avenues of life."

"Satan is true to himself in trying to teach that it is right to tell a lie. You would hardly expect him to express himself differently when he has been in this business ever since he fell from Heaven. He lied to Eve in the garden of Eden; to Cain who slew his brother; and to the long line of patriarchs and prophets. He has become so proficient in this kind of business that he is called the 'Father of Liars.' In the preceding remarks the Devil says that, 'It is not the lying that hurts a person but only when the lie is found out.' What can be more false than such a statement? When a person wilfully tells a lie, even though the lie may never be found out, its horrible scar is left upon the soul and will work injury sometime or somewhere, somewhat after the manner that poison in the blood will come to the surface in one way or another."

"Satan also teaches that a person who tells the truth all the time will be in trouble over half the time. But he forgets to say that if a person should get into trouble by telling the truth, that he has a clear conscience and is not afraid to face anybody. Indeed the very opposite of what he teaches is true. *A person who tells a lie a part of the time is in trouble all the time*. It will not be long until good people will lose respect for him, and also his own heart will be filled with a meanness that will blacken all the blessings of life."

"There may be certain extreme cases, such as the one concerning the dead husband to which Satan makes reference, where misrepresentation may be an act of mercy. But always in such cases the misrepresentation is just for a moment, to be followed by the real truth. A person is in a tight strait for an argument when he must use such a circumstance to try to prove that lying is justifiable."

"The other instances cited by Satan are all born of Hell, and the man who will permit his conscience to be turned to the channel of lying with a good object in view, will finally become so steeped in his inward iniquity that he can commit grosser crimes without impunity. The Bible is clear on the subject of lying. It is there expressly forbidden and even if you should be called upon to suffer pain for truth's sake, you can feel assured that in the end your triumph will be the more glorious. Words uttered in truth are fitly spoken, and are like 'Apples of gold in pitchers of silver.'"

Little Sermons by Satan to Persuade People to Reject the Great Invitation

A certain rich man lived in a magnificent mansion on a hill near a great city. He had power to work all manner of miracles and to fulfill any of his purposes. With a kind heart he prepared a great supper and sent special messengers into all parts of the city to invite the poor, the crippled, the blind and anyone else who could be persuaded to come. In obedience to the order, one of the messengers went toward the city, and as he came nigh to it, he met a beggar who had no home, and seemingly no friends.

"I have good news to tell you," said the messenger.

"It will be the first good news I have heard in many a day, say on," replied the beggar.

"I have come to tell you that you are invited to a great supper, at the rich man's house on the hill."

"You're only fooling me," returned the beggar with a look of interest in his eye.

"I am telling you nothing but the truth. I was sent out for the special purpose of inviting such as you are.

"There is something out of gear. You don't 'spose that such a critter as I am would be wanted in a king's palace."

"Surely I am not mistaken. If you are willing to go, you may enjoy the feast, and in addition receive many blessings from the rich man."

"He met a beggar who had no home, and seemingly no friends."

"How could I have the face to go? Don't you know that I have a black name, and have committed all manner of sins. I might as well say that I am living in the lowest comer of society, and am nothing but scum, with rags on the edge of it. You can't expect me to go."

The messenger then offered one persuasion after another but all were of no avail.

Note: This beggar is a type of the sinner who thinks he is too wicked to go to Christ. Satan and many of his human agents make him believe that there is no hope for a great sinner like he is.

Another messenger, with staff in hand, walked down an alley and rapped at the door of a very humble cottage. He was admitted by the inmate, a poor widow, who had struggled against the hard turns of fate for many a year. She had arisen from her grinding, to greet the messenger.

"I have joyful news to relate. You are invited to the king's palace on the hill, to partake of a great supper, which is now prepared."

"My friend, you have stopped at the wrong door, or perhaps you are looking for another person who bears my name."

"Surely I am not mistaken," insisted the messenger. "You are included amongst the number to whom I was sent with the invitation."

The messenger invited the poor widow to the great supper in the King's palace.

"Can you not see," still further replied the widow, "that I live in a broken-down house, and this, my best apparel, would not be acceptable in the eyes of a king. I should feel very much out of place if I would even try to accept the invitation."

Then did the messenger inform the poor widow that the king wished her to come just as she was, and that she would receive not only good things from the table, but beautiful raiment, and a clean heart.

The widow was moved to tears by this large offer. She spoke deep words of appreciation as she thought of her unworthiness of so great an honor. After a brief pause she encouraged the messenger by her acceptance of his invitation.

"I have decided to go, and you may look for me before the day is ended."

The messenger departed with a glad heart, after which the widow hurried to tell her neighbors of the great honor bestowed upon her, and of her intention to accept it.

Some of her friends rejoiced and urged her to go, while others made light of the whole affair, telling her that no one but a fool would think of doing what she was contemplating. Then she returned to her home with a sad heart and sat brooding over the discouraging words of her neighbors. In this manner she passed the hours and missed the great supper.

Note: This woman is a type of those sinners who are willing to accept salvation, but who are discouraged by companions and friends.

Another messenger, who was traveling through the city, met a wicked young man, and told him that he was invited to a feast at the rich man's house on the hill.

"What care I for a feast," said the young man. "So far in life I have had all I wish. If I were in need, I might accept this invitation, but indeed I have as good a feast as I want."

"Don't talk so foolhardy," said the messenger. "Your present feast is composed of poisonous foods, while that to which I invite you is life-giving and soul-healing."

"Don't you go," said some of the neighbors. "You will only make a fool of yourself."

"The young man haughtily tossed his head and passed on."

"You may mean it all well, but I prefer the bill-of-fare down here in the city, above that which can be found on the hill." So saying, the young man haughtily tossed his head and passed on.

Note: This young man is a type of the sinner who thinks he is having a better time in ungodliness than he could have by walking in the ways of truth.

One of the other messengers stopped at the home of a cripple, and upon entering, he informed the unfortunate man that he was invited to a splendid feast at the rich man's house on the hill.

"I know whom you mean," said the cripple. "I had often hoped that I might some day stand in the palace of the king, but by reason of my affliction I can never expect to travel so far."

"Is it your wish to go?" earnestly inquired the messenger.

"It is my whole heart's wish," replied the cripple.

"Then you shall reach the king's palace," assured the messenger.

"How can it be true that the rich man desires me to come as helpless as I am?" quickly asked the cripple.

"There is no mistake about it."

"But how can I reach the palace on the hill?"

"I will now give you all needed assistance."

At this the cripple's eye brightened, and after giving a second consent, the strong arms of the good messenger were employed in assisting the weak cripple through the streets of the city, and up toward the beautiful mansion. As they were passing through the gate towards the door of the palace, the rich man saw the cripple and hastened to greet him. At the foot of the beautiful steps took place the royal welcome, and a wonderful change in the cripple. He was made whole in an instant and he leaped joyously around the rich man's palace. Furthermore he was clothed with new garments, and with a most happy heart, he entered and partook of the feast.

Note: This cripple is a type of the sinner in bondage who joyfully receives the tidings of salvation, and gladly accepts the assistance that is offered by God's people.

The messengers went to all parts of the city and extended the invitation to everyone, although very few accepted. Each person who rejected gave one excuse or another. Others were so busily engaged with the pressing cares of life, that they gave no heed to the blessed invitation. But after they, who had accepted the invitation, had reached the king's palace, they had a most glorious time.

The King of Heaven extends an invitation to all people in the world to-day, inviting them to the gospel feast, which is richly supplied with the bread of life and the fruits of salvation. How have you acted toward this blessed invitation!

The rich man's house on the hill beautifully represents the Heavenly Father's house. No matter how terribly one is crippled with sin or groaning under the yoke of Satan, if such a one will go to the Heavenly Father he will be cured of all his spiritual ailments and relieved of the galling yoke. And moreover he will be clothed with the beautiful garments of salvation. The one who helps a single soul to such a happy state will be blessed with joy unspeakable, and shall finally share in all the glories of the Heavenly mansions.

The missionary led the cripple to the steps of the palace where he was made whole, and afterward clothed with new garments.

Satan, in artful disguise, is ever leading a host on the monotonous rounds of sin. He sings in his deceptive song that they who follow him will find the Living Spring, but the bones along the way tell more truly what their end will be.

Satan's Musical Sermon

As I looked out over the great highway of human life, I beheld an immense concourse of people who were passing along a smooth broadway, guided by one who appeared to be a royal leader, but who in reality was Satan himself. The famous leader was so artfully disguised that very few persons were able to detect his real nature. As Satan moved on at the head of this vast procession, he kept time with his musical instrument as he sang the following song:

"Come join our ranks as on we go,
To seek the living spring;
Where naught but healing waters flow,
Come, join our ranks and sing."

" 'Twill not be long ere you shall see
The fountain bubbling bright;
And he who quaffs its waters free,
Will revel in delight."

On either side of the wide path that ran in the form of a great circle, could be seen the bones and skulls of the millions who had already fallen from the ranks and perished by the wayside. This awful picture had but little effect upon the singers who ever continued in their monotonous rounds like willing slaves, or like sheep being led unconsciously to the slaughter.

It was nothing uncommon to hear a person calling from the wayside: "I thirst, where can I find the water of life?" And then to hear some one reply:

"Come with us for we are also seeking and hope to find the spring that will quench our thirst." In all probability the anxious creature would join the company in full hope of finding the spring. Each one of the large company had gone through the same experience as this earnest inquirer, and they are now all moving onward, blind leaders of the blind.

By way of truth it must be said that now and then some of these pilgrims lend a listening ear to the voices of love that are ever calling to those who travel in the monotonous rounds of sin, and by thus heeding the voice of warning they run to the shining path "That shineth more and more unto the perfect day," and where one can partake of the water of life as often and as freely as he wishes.

Those who follow Satan in this monotonous round are not only from the low walks of life, but you will find men and women of refinement and who possibly bear a good name in the community in which they live. Some of these followers are men of wealth and social influence; others are from the slum level of society, and still others are from the great host of the middle class of people. Here their elbows jostle one against another in the same giddy rounds of sin, each one ever trying to satisfy his thirst, and yet with each repeated round he finds his thirst more craving than before.

Here we see a picture of social inequality in natural life and of common equality in the service of Satan. They all meet the demands of the same leader, and are bound together by the same ties of infernal kinship.

What power can break the charm that Satan thus holds over these followers? The deceived hosts are walking as if in their sleep, and the large majority of them do not fully realize their condition until the roar of the great Niagara of death reaches their ears. Then some struggle in terror to escape the inevitable, but when persons are so near to the falls, it is next to impossible to rescue them.

By a little reflection one can easily see the emptiness of sin. The man who steps to the music of the Devil is indeed walking on the old, old path of sin all the time. He imagines that he is seeing the most up-to-date things as he walks after this deceptive leader. But let it be known that sin has nothing new to offer to its followers. It presents the same old sins that have been used by Satan from the beginning of the world. Talk about a theatre giving the same show for several hundred nights in one city, that is nothing compared to the program that the Devil offers to many a man, which is virtually the same, for over two score years. The only thing that appears new is the dress in which the sins are masked. The naked sin itself, if it could be photographed, would look alike in every century of human progress.

By the use of music, deception, masks, temptations, lies, intimidation, the Devil expects to carry on his campaign of continuing his foolish, yet terrible march on the highway of sinful circles. No doubt there will always be some, and altogether too many, who will follow him, but let those whose eyes are open to see the folly of the whole situation step from the sickening ranks, and take a firm foothold on the path of peace and righteousness, where the truest kind of progress can be made.

Satan on Child Training

"There is certainly a wrong opinion prevailing among some people regarding the early training of a child. Even though the world is several thousand years old, yet people will not learn by the follies of the past. A child is the greatest bundle of possibilities in the world, and we cannot expect the best results to follow if the mind of the child is spoilt during the first seven years of its existence."

"If you notice the policy which is pursued by some parents and guardians, you would infer that the child must be filled with all kinds of moral lectures and religious nonsense, until he groans under the terrible weight. To compel a child against it will to go to Sunday School or church before it is seven years old, is about the best way to ruin its mind for life."

"One of the first requisites of a good mental training is to teach self-dependence, and, as quickly as possible, get the individual to see things for himself. If it be your fond desire to have the child go to religious services, let the influence of a good example draw him, and not the severity of the rod or the sharp lectures from the lips."

"Allow a child to enjoy its natural liberty so that its expansion may be full and free. There is plenty of time for the weightier things, if the child's life is spared. The first seven years should be free from toil and restraint of any kind, except what the child may choose. In this manner the child will soon regard work as a pleasure. Think of the terrible effect it must have on a child's mind to put it into early slavery under a rod of fear. In this manner it is taught that life is a burden and that liberty, if it is to be enjoyed, must be a stolen pleasure."

"It would be better to keep a child out of Sunday School until he is seven years of age, and then allow him to go if he chooses. Constantly tell him, by your actions and your words, that religion is not intended to give a man greater liberty than he would otherwise enjoy, but on the contrary it often tends to narrow a man down to a set of hard rules. If religion were properly taught, it would have a wholesome effect upon the human race, but taught as it is in many places, it throws a dark gloom over what ought to be the brightest walks of life."

"Regarding the home instruction, a parent ought to be especially careful to impress upon the mind of a child nothing concerning the unseen world. Take the first seven years to teach a child concerning the things which he can see, hear and touch. Let him become thoroughly acquainted with the world of sense and sight before you attempt to launch him into that mystical realm of the unseen. You must not attempt too much during one period of life. Attend to one thing well and see to it that genuine development is reached. If this advice is adopted you will find, at the end of seven years, a child with a fine body, healthy in all of its parts which will be a mighty foundation upon which a wise instructor can nobly build."

"The great majority of people in this age of the world are determined to follow in the rut, and because their predecessors practiced the cramming method in the education of children, so they imagine that they must do likewise. What the world needs at this time is a number of reformers who will have the boldness and courage to teach the benefits of the method I have just advanced. Then, under the new teaching, the body will not be sacrificed for the sake of the mind, but the mind will begin to expand in the proper realm at the proper time. Then we shall see the beginning of the brightest era since the creation of the world. Until then let each one strive to fulfill the law as here advanced, and the great reward is sure to come.

A Brief Reply to the Preceding Sermon on Training Children

If the Devil would tell the truth, he would teach much differently on this subject than he has expressed in this preceding sermon. Satan knows that the first seven years of a child's life is very important in the shaping of its character. He also knows that if a child is not placed under control during this first period, that it will be almost impossible to control it afterward.

The teaching of Satan regarding the development of the body to the exclusion of the spiritual training during the first years of a child's life, is senseless and not worthy of attention. We believe that the body should be developed without impairing the mental faculties, and also that the soul should have a healthy growth without interfering with the natural body. There is no better time in life to leave deep impressions on a child's mind, than during the first part of its existence. Then you can teach it concerning the existence of a supreme being, and of the immortal life.

No child should be allowed to do as it pleases unless it pleases to do right. A boy or girl must early learn to be submissive to the will of another. If this is not learned its life will be more dangerous than a ship without an anchor on a stormy sea. Satan knows very well that if a child is not submissive to its parents, or to the true God, that he himself will gain control over its life.

Satan uses some beautiful expressions to show the outcome of his teachings, if they were observed. All this promise of a happy end is a wicked phantom, and is as untrue as Satan himself. He borrowed a picture of the Millennial Dawn and used it totally out of its connection.

The most distressing feature of the situation is this: there are many people who follow the teachings of Satan in full or in part. We hope that they will turn a deaf ear to the enemy and give their children the training that will bring the highest possible results.

Satan on Christian Zeal

A short sermon addressed to church-members, who are determined to travel the path of the just that shineth more and more unto the perfect day.

"Since you have surrendered yourself to God you have reached the highest possible condition of the spiritual life. What a pleasure it must be for you to stand on the mountain top where you can catch the Heavenly gales. Now you can enjoy the happy experience of being perfect, in which state you will have nothing more to strive after. Your main duty hereafter will be to see that decency and order prevail in the church. Do not allow yourself to be ruled by some dyspeptic preacher, who may urge you to continue struggling toward higher ground, fighting unreal foes until you breathe your last breath. Why not be satisfied with your glorious attainments, and take a rest? That is what

God wishes for you in the lovely passage: 'There remaineth therefore a rest to the people of God.' If you were a creature of the world, then you should not rest, but keep on struggling until you surrender to God. If you are a good Christian, you need not be afraid of temptations or anything of that kind. Suppose you should happen to yield to sin for a season, it could not have any bad effect upon you for God will keep you pure. Always remember that the Lord keeps his children in the hollow of his hand, and that nothing can harm them there."

"You may sin whenever you aim to do right through it. Your intentions will save you much more surely than your deeds. 'For as a man thinketh in his heart, so is he.' What has the outward deeds to do with a man's destiny, so long as he believes right in his heart!"

"You can see this truth demonstrated in the lives of all the great men of the Bible. If God had judged Daniel, Solomon and Peter by their outward deeds, not one of them would have reached Heaven. God, in his mercy, looked upon their hearts, and so they were enabled to stand in their evil day."

"Your greatest battle must be fought with those who misjudge you. Perhaps it may be a preacher or a Christian who makes a loud profession, and who is far beneath you in purity of character. 'Let none of these things move you.' Be like Paul;— stand firm on the rock, no matter who assaults you. 'Let your light so shine before men that they may see your good works and glorify your father which is in Heaven.' In time you will outlive the envy of your contemporaries, and the censure of your foes."

Comments on the Foregoing Sermon

One would hardly believe that any professing Christian would give heed to such ideas as Satan advances in the foregoing sermon. The Devil holds more than a dozen different views on one subject, each one to suit a different class of characters in life with which he may happen to deal. Yet there are thousands of church-members who give heed to his deathly doctrines, and although they are sinning without repentance, they make themselves believe that they have a clear conscience. How shrewdly Satan quotes scripture out of its real connection, and makes it convey a very false meaning. How easy it is for a Christian to fold his arms and do nothing. It is well for all persons who are tempted to a life of Christian ease to read the immortal lines of the poet:

"Must I be carried to the skies.
   On flowery beds of ease,
While others fought to win the prize,
   And sailed through bloody seas?"

Or read from the greatest of all books:
   "Woe to them that are at ease in Zion."

Let no one believe that indifference does not breed death. It must be avoided like a deadly serpent, for it eateth as doth a canker. The motto of the Christian ever should be to reach higher ground, and he should not be led to think that he will ever reach such a state in this life, from which he cannot make advancement.

Harmlessness of Sin – An Object Sermon by Satan

Once upon a time, Satan addressed an audience of worldly-minded Christians. He had prepared himself with objects by which to make a deeper impression of what he wished to teach. In one hand he held a branch of a fruit tree, that had been partly eaten by worms, but which contained good clusters of fruit. In the other hand, he held a beautiful branch on which the mark of the worm pest could not be seen, but this branch had no fruit.

"I appear to you this day to teach you the truth regarding the results of sin. You have heard it said that all sin is harmful. But I have come to tell you differently. A little sin becomes stimulating and works to a good end. Look at this fruit-bearing branch which I hold in my hand. It has been attacked by little worms until their marks of destruction are plainly visible all over it. Yet this has only stimulated the life of the branch, so that it has borne fruit abundantly. The best fruit in life is borne in sin, therefore I would urge you not to be afraid of certain small sins. You can see that the other branch has been free from the enemy's blight, and yet it has borne nothing but leaves."

"This fruitless branch is a fair sample of those people who want to be so pious and goody goody in life. They make a beautiful showing, but bear no fruit. As you walk along the pathway of life, you will notice that the best results come, not only from pure illumination, but by the mingling of the lower light with the higher. It is a case of two opposites flashing together to form the vital spark. Only as the soul is touched by sin can it reach its highest level. This does not necessarily mean that sin must predominate. One must learn how to live and serve a noble purpose, and at the same time entertain a little sin in his heart. I trust that you will leave this room to-day with broader views of life, and that you will not despise all sin because certain ones have such a black color."

A Reply to Satan's Talk on the Harmlessness of Sin

Since sin entered into the world its nature has not changed. Its tendency is always toward destruction and death, and it pollutes the soul just as the decayed part of an apple infects the whole of it. The Bible uses the strongest language to describe the terribleness of sin and its consequences. No poet or prose writer has ever been able to unfold the withering effects of sin which act upon the soul like poison upon the body.

45

Satan may point to the fruitless branch, and, by telling a lie, try to teach that lack of fruit is due to the healthy condition of the tree, but such deception will not go very far with sensible people. Every person knows that the first requisite to fruit-bearing is a good condition of the trunk and branches of the tree. If a worm-eaten branch bears fruit, the fruit grows in spite of the worms and not because of them. Satan is true enough when he insinuates that the worm bears the same relation to the tree that sin does to the character of a person. Follow out this fact and see the blighting effects of waste and ruin on one tree after another. Many valuable trees commence to die just because the worms are eating the life out of them, and if their course is not checked certain death will come to the trees. So in a similar manner will sin work its ruin, if it is allowed to operate upon a single soul. A small portion of it is of the same quality as the large consignments. It all comes from the same black bottle of death, and if Satan were truthful he could unfold a tale of horrors concerning the effects of sin that would shudder any human being.

The Lord's Supper

Sermon delivered to an inquiring mind that had been staggering under doubt for a long time. Satan appeared and addressed his subject as follows:

"I am happy to see you this morning so profitably engaged in reading the Bible. This is an evidence of your sincerity, and a proof that you will have a greater interest in what I am about to utter. I feel that it is my duty to tell you some of the latest truths on the subject of the Lord's Supper. If you will give me your closest attention so as to fully understand me, I am certain that you will receive much good, for there is no doubt about the correctness of my views according to common sense and the Bible. You need not expect me to give you the same old antiquated doctrines that have warped the spiritual eyesight of Christian's for nineteen hundred years, but I purpose to give you some truths thoroughly up-to-date. Let me first tell you something about the

Purpose of Instituting the Lord's Supper

"There is no mystery about this inasmuch as Christ clearly stated his purpose. 'This do in remembrance of me.' Some men perpetuate their memory by building institutions of learning, others by endowing hospitals and establishing libraries, and still others by their illustrious deeds in peace or in war. But Christ, more wise than all his followers, simply commanded that men should gather together and honor him by a simple and inexpensive service."

"At the time when the Lord's Supper was instituted no one dreamed that the command of Christ referred to any one except his immediate disciples. To them this rite was obligatory. It would be most interesting history to explain how the custom of drinking wine and eating bread as an act of worship was continued beyond the apostolic age, but let us waste no time in stumbling over the rocky paths of early church history; we must face the situation as it is in this present age."

"As you take a close observation of the followers of Christ, you will see that they are divided into several classes. One class observes this so-called ordinance in a purely formal manner, and for no other reason than that they have seen others observing it as far back as they can remember. Another class of Christians, as they look at this subject, are fully awake to the customs of the ages, but they are still more alive to the Bible itself. How refreshing it is to find a Christian who is able and willing to take a broad view of each doctrine in the Bible! Has it ever occurred to your mind that the real truth of scripture is contrary to any service that has the appearance of the so-called Lord's Supper? But you must remember that it requires a truly enlightened mind and a courageous heart to accept and practice such up-to-date truth."

"It is not necessary to enter into a lengthy discussion concerning this question. Allow me simply to say that Christ spoke to his disciples only, and was making arrangements for their social union. This was perfectly proper and it served to bind these immediate followers into one humble fraternity. It is true that they gathered together and ate bread from one loaf and drank wine from one cup and otherwise entered into worship and honored the memory of the suffering and death of their Master. All this was in strict obedience to the spoken command of their recently living Lord."

"Now let me repeat that there is not a single passage in the whole Bible that commands the perpetual observation of this ordinance. Then why should you linger in doubt and thus torment your mind on this misunderstood question? Come out into the clear light and enjoy the greater liberty which is promised to all those who prefer to follow the Bible rather than the whims and fancies of its blind devotees."

"Next let me consider the attitude of Christians to-day toward this subject. It may not be a sin to observe this antiquated custom, but it is certainly not required. Let each one be bold enough to come out on the side of truth, and although the great majority may be slow in changing yet let those who are more enlightened and more truth-loving, step out first. Under any circumstances you must be charitable toward those who insist upon observing the Lord's Supper. Always remember that many have been so trained from their youth up, and if they were to cease observing this rite it would only make them feel miserable."

"I would also give you some advice that will be of good service to you as you come in contact with those who believe and practice this doctrine. First of all discourage as much as possible the exercising of any emotional spirit. It is bad enough to become enthusiastic over the best part of religion, but it is much worse to show the color of emotion over the imaginary features of the faith. Away with all fanaticism. The Lord's Supper will never die out as long as it is made the occasion of melting hearts into one spirit of rejoicing, or of tears."

"If a church or people insist upon a frequent observance of this so-called ordinance, use your strongest influence to make it the most formal and dignified of all the forms of worship. If there is any place where a man or woman needs a cool head it is in religion. If he is not calm and steady, he is liable to flounder like the unhappy and unfortunate fish out of its natural element."

"I will further advise you to be bold in your teaching on the kind of emblems to be used in the celebration of the Lord's Supper. Spend your influence to get the church to use the most harmless ingredients. Either common sense or a liberal education will teach that the emblems of the Eucharist can be changed to suit the climate and also the custom of the people. There is no necessity of clinging to bread and wine, as if nothing else could be figurative of Calvary's tragic scenes. If you were in China, what would be more appropriate than rice and water? In Germany what would be more fitting than pretzels and beer? In America crackers and grapes would be very suitable emblems."

After Satan had finished his sermon, he left to plant his seeds of error in some other heart.

Some Things which Satan Failed to Mention in the Foregoing Sermon

1. He neglected to say with certainty that Christ being the Son of God, was the center of all authority.

2. He also placed a false and selfish construction on the words: "This do in remembrance of me."

3. It is certain that the command to observe the Lord's Supper pointed away to the churches of all ages, because the observance continued from the first apostles to all Christians at once. This would not have been probable if the sacred supper were intended only for the apostles.

Also if we localize the command concerning the Lord's Supper, so must we localize the sermon on the mount and the greater part of the New Testament.

4. Concerning the emblems; Satan forgot to say that Christ selected these, and it is not left to the whims and fancies of the people of any nation or any climate to select as they may choose. Satan well knows that if he could persuade people to change the emblems at will, that he has won a very decisive victory against the Lord's Supper.

Family Worship

A Modern Sermon by Satan on the Foolishness of Religious Services in the Home. Delivered to a Christian Father and Overheard by a Company of Evil Spirits

"I have come to you on this occasion to enlighten your mind regarding the custom of family worship. After careful consideration of the subject I am firmly convinced that family worship is the most useless of all the forms of religious service. A family should not be selfish in its devotion, when an opportunity is at hand to attend public services. The practice of family worship may have been all right in an age when there were few churches or at the present time in communities where people live in isolated homes. But, where churches are within reach of the families I can see that more harm than good is accomplished by holding home worship of any kind."

"One of the main reasons why family worship is useless, is not alone because of an abundant supply of churches, but because of the great variety of services that are held in them on the Sabbath day and throughout the week. It is much better to be faithful to some of these general meetings of the church, than to spend so much of your valuable time in the home worship that must of necessity become monotonous."

"This is a sharp age of competition, and when a man awakes from his sleep with fresh energy, it is his duty to go into the regular work of the day with all the push possible. He owes his best working hours to the support of his family, and to the duty which he must perform to his fellow creatures. It may be all right for a lazy man or a man who has no work to do, to stay at home in the morning and hold family services of ten minutes or more."

"Then in the next place, where is there any necessity for family worship? People are not bad because they don't know any better. The family worship does not add anything to the instruction imparted in the church, and therefore it is useless. People are smarter in these days than they were in the older times, consequently they need not consult headquarters so often. In the age of persecution, it must be admitted, that family worship was a great comfort, and it proved to be a strong staff in the time when sharp trials had to be borne. But now, when people are more charitable, and when liberty of conscience is established, there is no further need to maintain the home worship. Let each one do his praying privately. It will be a great accomplishment if even that much is done."

"Church members ought to know how many children are influenced against religion by compelling them to gather in worship once or twice a day with a father and mother whose home life has no doubt been more or less stormy. In many instances the mother has told the children white and black lies and then gets down to pray before them, or perhaps the father has been living somewhat inconsistently and the children hear him act the part of a saint in his morning or evening prayer."

Then Satan whispered to his imps unheard by the man: "It does not take very long for the children to see that religious devotion and a crooked life can be hitched together. Then when the children grow older they will perhaps have an impression that any kind of a life will do to be a Christian." Satan turning again to the man, continued:

"The average parent at best is very poorly qualified to impart religious instruction. This is one of the greatest reasons why there should be no attempt made to hold religious services in the home, or to impart any kind of scriptural instruction there. All such work should be left to those who are more competent. The children will then get less instruction, but it will go much farther in its good results."

"The best kind of family worship is that in which the father and mother and the children show the proper kind of love and respect for one another and in all things, as much as possible, follow the dictates of a good conscience."

"If I had my own way, I would break down all the family altars in the land. If I could not persuade the children to go to church, I would not compel them, but I would wait until they were old enough to see the benefit of it. In that way the child would be religious of his own free choice, and that would count for more good than for him to be a Christian by compulsion."

This address was very much appreciated by the company of imps who heard it, for some of them were running short of ammunition. Certain ones of the chief spirits present declared that the speech was thoroughly up-to-date, and that it would be used with good effect to pull down some of the family altars.

A Reply to Satan on Family Worship

It is easily understood why Satan is so strongly opposed to family worship. Anything of this kind, which is so pleasing to God, and so profitable to the members of the family, is certainly very damaging to the kingdom of Satan. If Satan could destroy religion in the home, he would then laugh to see the last flickering of the religious fires in the world.

Satan and his followers argue that there is no necessity for family worship on account of the many services held in the churches. They might as well argue that there is no necessity for the little rills of water that run into the spring inasmuch as there is so much water in the spring. The spring would soon dry up if its feeders were once closed, so would the life of church services become dead and formal if the Christian life of the individual in the home would come to an end.

Satan also argues that a busy man has no time to hold family worship. This would be true if family worship were worthless, but when we consider what effect it has on the members of the home, we can form a clearer idea of its great value. It binds the hearts of the parents closer together and they feel that God has a part in the rearing of the children. Also the children have a greater respect for the heads of the home, and on their young minds are fixed eternal impressions for good. The power and influence of religious services in the home reach far beyond the limit of the family circle, which could be proved by a long list of incidents.

Satan also argues in the preceding sermon that there is no necessity for family worship because the church furnishes ample instruction. We certainly rejoice in the fact that the church furnishes so much good instruction, and this is a splendid help to the upbuilding of religious thought and character. Any wise parent should know how to make the best use of this church help. But the best fruit is produced by personal care, by a loving interest on the part of the parents in the home. The world can never tell the amount of good that has been accomplished around the family altar, in conjunction with which all other good influences will harmonize into the perfecting of the individual life and character.

We hope the time will never come when Satan's ambition will be realized. We believe that he would rejoice very much if every family altar could be broken down. It should therefore be a pleasure to everybody to uphold the holy influence of the home altar, and thereby do something for the betterment of mankind and toward the overthrow of the kingdom of darkness.

Satan and Purity

Preached by Satan to a Young Lady at one of the By-ways of Life

A certain young lady who was traveling along the pathway of Purity, felt the pulse of temptation at a certain place where steps of Prostitution led downward to one side of the path. As if held by some strange magic, she paused, scanned the steps and was inclined to descend, yet her better judgment forbade her. Then the invisible Satan spoke to her mind through that wireless telegraphy long ago known to the spirits:

"You have come to an important turn in your experiences. If you descend these steps you will taste of life's fruit for the first time. Nature has called you to walk downward here, and after you have passed over these steps you will gain the new knowledge, which will open your eyes to the broadest views of life. True enough the advice of your mother and father forbid you to pursue such a course, but it is well known that loving parents, in their zeal to do good, go to wide extremes in advising their children. Your mother knows that you are entitled, by the grant of nature, to the blessed fruit that can only be found on the lower level."

The young lady answered in her own soul: "I cannot go by the way of these steps. The time has not yet arrived for me to seek or enjoy such privileges which are contrary to the customs of goad society, and at variance with the laws of God."

"Nonsense! Nonsense!" came the suggestion from Satan. "The time to eat fruit is when you have an appetite for it, and the most charming appetite is the first. Some of the wisest of the world have improved the golden opportunity, and descended these steps at your very age of life. Why should you hesitate! Virtue, if once lost, can easily be regained, and it is a thousand times better to experience the sweet influence on this lower level, than to deny yourself day by day on the vain assumption that purity must be maintained at any cost."

The Three Stages of Prostitution

The young lady felt in her soul that this teaching came from the enemy, then she passed through a mighty struggle with both the flesh and the Devil. She was conquering in the trying ordeal, and contrary to the wishes of Satan, she breathed her prayer to God for deliverance. The heroine broke away from the spell that seemingly bound her, and refused to listen any longer to the voice of temptation that would have blasted the flower of her purity, and without mercy send the cursed pangs of sin and regret into her soul.

As she passed on, the comfort of victory welled up within her, and her joy was unspeakable.

Satan used all kinds of arguments to persuade this young lady to descend to the lower level of prostitution. But she won the victory and continued on the path of Purity.

Satan, in the form of a hobgoblin, undertook to frighten Miss Pilgrim, who, quick as a flash, thrust her sword toward him. He escaped injury by throwing himself backward.

The Journey of Miss Pilgrim

During which Satan Delivered some Sermonets

A young lady whose ambitions were pure prayed for a good equipment instead of riches. In answer to her prayer she received a splendid outfit from the armory of God. On her head was a perfect helmet of salvation; her heart was protected by a shining breast-plate of righteousness, and her loins were girded about with truth. Also her feet were shod with the preparation of the gospel of peace, and in her left hand was a most beautiful shield of faith, while in her right hand she held a two-edged sword. When she had received this powerful outfit for attack and defence, she was exhorted to pray with all supplication and watch with all perseverance.

How beautiful she looked as she walked forth upon the way of life, ready to meet any foe and even prepared to conquer in any strife. But better than all, she was prepared to enjoy the scenery along the way, and to hold peaceful fellowship with the unseen God.

Now behold the evil one sought to overcome this fair young Pilgrim. He knew that it would be of no use to preach infidelity to her, as she was thoroughly informed in Bible truths. He closely followed her for many a day ever watching for some opportunity whereby he might win a victory over her.

As this young Pilgrim journeyed on, she found that the way was becoming more and more delightful to her, for it is true that they who travel diligently on the good path enjoy the greatest amount of happiness. One day as she was making splendid progress she came to a place where Satan, in the form of a terrible Hobgoblin, undertook to frighten her. He came upon her without notice, suddenly rushing down to the edge of the path on which she was traveling and shouting with all terror:

"Throw down that sword and shield or I will tear the heart out of you."

Quick as a flash, the young pilgrim nerved herself for an attack, and in swift defence she raised her shining shield and thrust her sword toward him as she uttered these words:

"In the name and by the help of the living God, I will keep my shield, my sword and my heart."

Had the monster not thrown himself backward, he would have suffered sharp pain from the sword of Miss Pilgrim. Her boldness totally baffled him, inasmuch as he did not raise his bludgeon which he had left fall during her attack. He well knew that he could wage no successful battle with her as long, as she remained on the path of righteousness. So he changed his tactics and suddenly made himself more beautiful, and with pleasing address he tried to decoy her to one side, but she was shrewd enough not to step on forbidden ground. After a series of vile but futile efforts the transformed Hobgoblin gathered himself together and disappeared.

When this mean attack by Satan was ended, Miss Pilgrim rejoiced with joy unspeakable and full of glory. She praised God for the strength with which she was blessed to conquer so completely. Then she sung some of the good songs of Zion, and drank anew of the water of life, and ate a goodly portion of a spiritual feast which had been provided for her. After this she found that her path led through a pleasant woodland, where flowers grew on either side of the way, and where sweet birds sang most charmingly. She testified to many of her friends that this was the most delightful spot which she had yet reached since she put on the whole armor of God.

Miss Pilgrim found no lack of company, and the fellowship of saints was so enjoyable to her that she prayed more earnestly than ever for those who were deceived so much that they imagined the company of the Broad Highway to be more congenial than any other.

Now it happened that Miss Pilgrim, in her journey entered into a peculiar country where temptations abound. Although she knew the character of Satan and his manner of working, yet she was not aware that he was following her so closely. The Evil One noticed a suitable place ahead to which he hastened, so as to reach it before Miss Pilgrim. When she approached him she noticed an angel-like form, but upon closer inspection she was positive that it was the enemy in disguise.

"Pause a moment," said the angel-like creature, "allow me to ask you how much you will take for the helmet which you have on your head?"

"I will not part with it under any circumstances," she answered with determination.

"I will give you a crown of pure gold in exchange, if you will surrender it," calmly offered the Tempter.

"Of what use is a crown to me now? I look for a crown at the end of my race. This is the day of helmet wearing, because I cannot tell what moment some fiery darts may be hurled at me."

"Ha! ha!" laughed the Tempter, "I can see that you have been deceived. You have fought your battles well and it will hardly happen that you will need the helmet any more this side of Heaven's gate. On account of your faithfulness, I have been sent to crown you. Why should you hesitate to accept your reward which will be a thousand times more beautiful than the rough helmet now on your head, and more than that, this crown will be more suited to your grace of body, and your peculiar charms."

The young lady scanned for a moment the bright object in the hand of the angel-like creature, and then said that she had received explicit orders not to surrender her helmet until she had reached the very gate of Heaven. "Then," she said, "I will lay my armor down, and not before that time."

Then the enemy, with artful conversation, continued his temptations, and the young pilgrim firmly resisted them all. After a short season had passed, she poised her sword steadily and demanded that she be disturbed no longer. She escaped without a battle, and went on her way rejoicing.

After the lapse of a few days, when she had quite forgotten her last temptation, she was again traveling alone in her usual manner, when she met another peculiar object that looked more like an angel than a devil.

"Hold on, my young friend!" cried out a voice, "I am so glad that you came along just at this time. I am in great need of a shield as I must travel a path where fiery darts are hurled. If you will do me the great favor of loaning your shield to me I will return it in good order and will be under infinite obligations to you."

This tender, pathetic appeal touched the heart of Miss Pilgrim more than any other form of temptation which she had yet encountered, but she quickly remembered what had been said to her: "Let no man take thy shield," and looking toward the Tempter's face, she answered:

"This shield is not my own. I am forbidden to part with it under a severe penalty."

"Surely no harm can come to you, for your journey is over a smooth country where no foes abound. Before you will need it, I will return it again into your hands."

It happened that the young soldier thoughtlessly dropped her shield a little during this conversation, and the Tempter being convinced that he could not persuade her to surrender it, made an ugly attack upon her with a handful of fiery darts, some of which flew over the top of her shield and struck her helmet.

"Ah!" she quickly cried, "how thankful I am that I did not give my helmet for the crown." After this she made a bold attack upon the foul demon, who, observing that his fiery darts had done her no harm, quickly made good his escape.

Miss Pilgrim, as she continued on the King's Highway, came to a place where she heard strange music from some unknown source. Being a lover of music she paused to listen, and as she listened, she was quite captured by the beautiful strains, and she found herself being drawn toward the place whence came such unusual melodies. Miss Pilgrim was so enraptured that she did not think that she was treading on dangerous ground, nor were her suspicions aroused until she fell through a layer of dead twigs and leaves into a pit. It was a miracle that she was not bruised by her fall. Before she had time to examine the pit she was confronted by a polite gentleman, who seemed to approach her through an underground passage.

"Happy to see you."

Miss Pilgrim made no reply. As yet she had no time to collect her thoughts.

"How came you into this place!"

"I fell into it by accident," explained Miss Pilgrim as her fears were increasing.

"And shall I help you out?"

"If you please, sir."

"Follow me and I will take you to a place where there are steps leading to the sunlight."

Miss Pilgrim commenced to pray for direction and seeing no possible way to get out by the way she came in, she was compelled to follow her would-be rescuer. She was fully conscious of his evil designs, and being caught so innocently, she was determined to make the best possible escape from her sudden captivity.

Mr. Polite conducted Miss Pilgrim through a winding underground channel and came to a room dimly lighted. Here he paused and turning to her he calmly requested:

"Lay down your weapons and enjoy a rest."

"That would be signing my death-warrant," she answered with decision.

At this Mr. Polite turned the key, thereby locking the only door to the room. Miss Pilgrim now took a bold stand and drew her sword.

"My God is able to deliver me from your foul hands. I charge you to open that door, or take the edge of this blade."

"Be not so enraged, my friend, I closed that door only to keep out a set of mean fellows who would have forcibly torn your weapons and your honor from you."

Then quick as a flash, Mr. Polite opened the door and rushed out, closing and locking the door after him.

Left to herself Miss Pilgrim spent her time in prayer. She was confronted by an angel who told her to wait for the time of her deliverance, and meanwhile trust in God. In a short time the keeper of the place entered, and told her that she would be liberally compensated at the end of her period of service.

"My period of service is already at an end. You shall not have my free will in sin a single moment," firmly and defiantly declared Miss Pilgrim.

The keeper approached her in silence and Miss Pilgrim suspecting his motive, drew her sword in defence: "I warn you not to touch me while I wield this sword," cautioned Miss Pilgrim with a firm voice.

The keeper suddenly halted and being enraged, he addressed the brave heroine: "How dare you flaunt a sword in my face?"

"Only in the name of Him whom I serve. I warn you again to lay no hand upon me."

"Do you not know, my young girl, that your life is in my hands? If I so choose I can put an end to you this very day."

"You speak a falsehood. You cannot put an end to me. You could easily tear this body of mine apart, or burn it, but you must not think that you could put an end to me. If you drag me down to death by sheer force, you will thereby give me a short route to Heaven. I will live forever after my body is cold in death."

"Ah, you are quite a preacher!" jestingly said the keeper. "You ought to be in the pulpit, not down here in a place like this."

The keeper tarried no longer but hurriedly left the room locking the door after him.

Miss Pilgrim continued in earnest prayer for deliverance from the foul place where she was held captive. Her prayer was one of submission, for she expressed her willingness to die if need be rather than surrender her faith.

A short time thereafter there appeared a gentleman of splendid physique and bearing a pleasant countenance. After he had entered the room he addressed Miss Pilgrim in a fascinating manner:

"I am indeed glad to meet you, my friend, I have come to spend a social hour with you."

"If you wish to hold conversation with me you must wait until I am free from this place. I am now in bondage."

"Are you not at liberty to do as you please?"

"I am a slave in bondage. I have no control over that door through which you have entered. I will have nothing to do with any man while I am in this low den. Once more I say that I will gladly speak with you if you see to it that I escape."

The winning man plied all his ingenuity to persuade the beautiful Miss Pilgrim to a violation of her honor, but she fought to the sword's point until the visitor, defeated and ashamed, left the room. After this manner Miss Pilgrim conducted herself until she was enabled to escape. She went forth most gladly into the welcome light of the King's Highway, and keenly remembered the music that pulled her feet from the proper path. She cautioned herself anew not to give heed to anything whatever that would tempt her from the path of life whereon she was traveling.

The King's Highway never appeared to her so handsome as now. The dark shadows of the den deepened her appreciation of the blessed light that Heaven was bestowing on her as she continued on her journey. Her eyes feasted anew on the unsurpassed scenery, and her prayers of gratitude ascended to Heaven with more fervor than ever.

Not long after this when Miss Pilgrim was meditating along the way, there was a dark being called Fear that rushed toward her like a cyclone, and instantly hurled many fiery darts, but they struck her shield and fell broken at her feet. Miss Pilgrim addressed this creature with great courage. Her experience with the Hobgoblin helped her greatly to meet this new foe.

"Away! away! you fearful creature. Neither you nor your darts can break in upon me, for I am under eternal protection as long as I retain these weapons."

The demon of Fear, finding that he could make no impression on Miss Pilgrim, drew himself to one side and the heroine sang more joyously than ever as she passed on.

Miss Pilgrim was now to meet one of her hardest temptations, because of the deceitful manner in which it came. As she was walking along, a beautiful young lady, of about her same age, stepped up along side of her from the rear, and without giving Miss Pilgrim time to observe the path whereon she had traveled, entered into conversation with her.

"Happy I am that I have found a companion so near my own age. I hope that we may be congenial to each other, so that we can travel this path together with mutual profit."

"Who are you, and whence came you?" asked Miss Pilgrim.

"I am a friend of yours from the same city whence you came, and I am traveling to the same Heaven to which you are going," came the response of the New-Comer.

"You have a strange outfit. How could you have traveled so far on this road without being harmed? Where are your equipments!"

"I keep them all concealed," came the reply, whereat the new companion revealed a sword from the loose folds of her garments," See! here is my sword. Let us exchange just for courtesy's sake."

"If you have used your sword so well up to this time, and I have used mine so well, it would be better for us to let well enough alone."

"You might as well be sociable and make the exchange," continued the New-Comer. "It may be that each of us can do still better with a new sword." Miss Pilgrim was almost in the act of complying with the evil request, when an inward voice gave her counsel: "Beware, lest any man take thy sword." The inward voice troubled her so much that she stoutly refused to think any further of making the exchange. The New-Comer, being angry at the failure to gain her point, kept watching for a good chance whereby she might rob Miss Pilgrim of her sword.

At a moment when Miss Pilgrim was unguarded the New-Comer seized her in a foul grasp, and was in the act of throwing her to the ground when she offered a stout resistance. Then followed a brief wrestling match in which no mercy was shown on either side. For a moment it appeared that Miss Pilgrim was overpowered, when she saw an opportunity and with her strong right arm she tore the very garments from the back of her assailant, and to her horror she discovered that the one who seemed to be Miss New-Comer was now revealed in his true light in devilish masculine attire. Miss Pilgrim having her loins girded with truth and having on the breastplate of righteousness, felt no harm from all the terrific blows, which the demon continued to deliver. In the midst of the hot affray Miss Pilgrim succeeded in striking one fatal blow with her sword. A sudden change took place, for the gasping, writhing form of her contemptible foe lay beneath her begging for mercy.

"You miserable wretch," cried Miss Pilgrim, "you deceiver, you liar; had you taken my sword, you would have laid me low. You deserve death, and if you were mortal I would put an end to you at once. How dare you defy one who is clad in the panoply of Almighty God? Taste this sharp edge once more," she shouted as she again thrust the two-edged blade through him.

A low groan and the victory was complete. After this terrible encounter Miss Pilgrim continued her journey more triumphant than ever. She soon overtook a friend who was sore depressed on account of the many troubles and persecutions through which he had passed. Mr. Depressed looked upon the cheerful face of Miss Pilgrim and inwardly prayed that he might learn the secret of her happiness. Miss Pilgrim, after her natural manner, commenced speaking words of cheer to her friend, who received them with a kindly spirit.

A conversation ensued in which Mr. Depressed related some of his recent experiences and then with an envious tone he asked the following question:

"Why is it, my friend, that you have such an easy time of it? Trouble seems to vanish at your appearance, and it seems that good luck is always standing around in your way."

"I fear that you are looking at me in a wrong light," smilingly replied Miss Pilgrim. "It has not been long since I passed through a deadly struggle and I have had many such experiences since I set out toward the gate of Heaven."

"Then why is it that you are not cast down?"

"Because I am obedient to the orders of my king. Under no circumstances will I surrender any part of my equipment. Thus determined I conquer every foe in the name of the living God. Surely I have all reason to rejoice when victory is mine."

"Have you given me the full secret of your peace and happiness?" further asked Mr. Depressed.

"The companions I have also help me to be happy and cheerful. I have the company of sweet angels who minister unto me day and night. If you could see them as they hover around me at times, your face would shine with a new light and your life would also be lived in the charmed circle."

"'Charmed circle,'" repeated Mr. Depressed. "Please give me more light on this."

"There is a charmed circle in life in which any one may live who wishes. No matter where they go the charm need not be broken, and rich supplies of blessings can always be had.

"Let me urge you to get into this circle and thereby learn the secret of a happy life: If you welcome the angels of mercy, comfort, peace, faith, hope, love and purity and a host of others, they will surround you and your life will be spent in the charmed circle."

Miss Pilgrim had no time to tarry longer. She hastened away to fill certain engagements. The influence of her few words upon Mr. Depressed had a wonderful effect, and one by one he welcomed the angels until he also realized the great happiness of living in the charmed circle.

The journey of Miss Pilgrim was long and interesting. It would take a whole book to tell the many experiences through which she passed before she came in sight of the gate of Heaven. She was a valiant soldier to the last and as she reached the gates of light she was covered with many a scar but was still in possession of her whole armor. A beautiful angel conducted her until the gates of Heaven swung ajar. Her entrance through the shining portals was most glorious and triumphant. A choir of angels sang her welcome home. After this the gate of Heaven closed and it was not seen what else occurred to her.

A beautiful angel conducted Miss Pilgrim until the gates of Heaven swung ajar. Her entrance through the shining portals was almost glorious and triumphant. A choir of angels sang her welcome home.

The farmer turned a deaf ear to the voice of Satan and went no farther than the fence. He yielded to an Angel of Light and returned to his home.

The hardships and trials of this mortal life will dwindle into insignificance when the day of victory comes. All the heavy burdens of the Christian will lose their weight in the light of Heaven's gate. Miss Pilgrim was a noble character who won her way by faith through all the sharp conflicts of life. How her heart was thrilled with joy as she saw the gates of Heaven open to her at the end of her journey. The angels that came to welcome her sang their sweetest celestial melodies. Such a glorious end will be experienced by each one who puts on the whole armor of God and goes forth with courage in the battle of right against wrong and of sin against darkness.

A Time when Satan Failed

The following narrative is taken from real life. The occurrence happened in a farming district in one of the populous counties of Pennsylvania.

Two men owned adjoining farms and they lived as neighbors for many years. During the first part of this period the relations between the two men and their families were pleasant, but unfortunately a bitter enmity arose between the two farmers, which continued from year to year until the situation became desperate.

During the period of this bitterness neither farmer L. nor farmer B. made the necessary advancements to settle the brewing difficulty. And so the feud continued to grow stronger and stronger until farmer B. secretly and quietly resolved to revenge his neighbor. All this was unknown to farmer L., who never went so far as to plan revenge.

One night, when the moon was peeping out between drifting clouds, farmer L. retired early, but for some reason his sleep had partly gone from him. In the deep hours of the night he arose from his bed and walked to the second story rear porch of his home, whence he glanced out upon the ever-changing scene in the Heavens. A moment later he dropped his eyes for a cursory glance across the indistinct fields, and to his surprise, he saw his neighbor B. walking slowly toward his barn. And just as plainly as he saw his neighbor he saw two companions with him, one seemed to be dressed in white garments and the other clothed in black. These two strange companions were unknown to farmer L. as he stood intently gazing upon the trio where he thought that he could not be seen by them. No one, under such circumstances, would turn away with indifference and enter the house, so he remained to watch what might be the outcome of the strange affair.

The trio slowly advanced and were seemingly engaged in a deep, quiet conversation. Farmer B., who walked in the middle, was earnestly besieged by his two companions. Each one seemed to be endeavoring to make the strongest impression upon him. In this strange manner the men continued until they came to the fence not far from the barn. Here they paused and apparently the conversation continued. Farmer L. was greatly perplexed at the strange occurrence, and was not able to advance any explanation that would satisfy his own mind. All he could do was to continue watching and waiting for developments.

In a short time, which seemed more like an hour than a few moments, the black companion slowly left the fence and walked alone across the field in a different direction from which the three had come. A moment later farmer B. started homeward accompanied by the white companion. Farmer L. watched the two until they were out of sight, and he tarried for several hours to see whether or not they would return. But nothing greeted his gaze except the faithful moon, drifting clouds and a night scene of the earth before him. Finally he returned to his couch and rested as best he could until daybreak, after which he arose and ate scantily of breakfast. He could not shake off the impressions of the preceding night, and after a few hours of restlessness, he decided to go over and speak to farmer B. about what he had seen under the light of the quarter moon.

Farmer B. received his neighbor and story with much surprise at first, and after a few moments he wept bitterly, and confessed to neighbor L. that in the wickedness of his heart, he had planned to set his barn on fire the night before. He declared that he kept his intentions a secret from everybody, even his own wife. Farmer B. then related how he proceeded across the field and was unable to go farther than the fence near the bam. Farmer L. then made inquiry concerning the two strange companions.

"What two companions," asked farmer B.

"The two men who were walking with you across the field."

"Do you mean last night?"

"Certainly."

"Have I not told you that I revealed my plans to nobody and that I went alone?"

"But I tell you in all honor that I saw two creatures with you. One was dressed in white and the other in black. You walked between them, and they seemed to engage your whole attention."

"Very strange! very strange!" said farmer B. "I surely know of no one who accompanied me."

Then farmer L. related again the whole story slowly and clearly, giving all the details. Everything corresponded exactly with the confession and memory of farmer B. except the part relating to the two companions. He admitted, however, that he was in a great war with his thoughts. At one moment some influence seemed to urge him to set the barn on fire, then suddenly he seemed to feel as if he ought to return home and not play the part of a mean incendiary. Between these two forces lie claimed that he pushed his way until he reached the memorable fence. Here he paused and entertained for the last time the idea of setting the barn on fire. He yielded to the nobler impulse and returned to his home.

Farmer B. was intensely thankful that he had yielded to the better impulse, and asked the pardon of his neighbor for the sin of even entertaining such an evil plot against him. The pardon was graciously granted, after which the two farmers were convinced that the companions of the night previous, were two representatives from the spirit world, one a good angel of mercy, and the other a wicked demon.

How to Conduct Revival Meetings

A Special Sermon by Satan to Church-Members in all parts of the Christian World.

"I am glad for the opportunity of telling you some up-to-date-truths regarding revival meetings. The history of the ages has proved that some of the methods of conducting revivals are not only weak but out of harmony with good taste. Enthusiasm has damaged the church through many of the world's ages, for you can safely conclude that when fanaticism runs away with any congregation, it is doomed to degenerate. The emotional spirit is more manifest among the less intelligent people, therefore we must not be too severe in criticising our fathers and mothers who, under Wesley and Whitfield, grew very demonstrative. It was very common in those days to hear people calling aloud for mercy and shouting, or shedding bitter tears of penitence. But thanks to a better age, we are not so much afflicted with such scenes, except in certain obscure comers. The church will reach the zenith of its glory only as it throws aside the sensational features of its worship."

"We should hail with delight the dawning of a better era when revivals will be conducted in a manner more pleasing to the cultured tastes of men. We need but look around us to see how rapidly these improved conditions are being adopted. Some churches are determined not to keep in step with progress, but there is hope that a new generation will be more refined."

"It is therefore the duty of every progressive church-member to discourage any of those old-time methods that put the church to ridicule before the best thinking people of the world. I feel it to be my duty to lay before you my opinion as to what is essential to promote an up-to-date revival."

1. "If you wish to promote a revival secure the best possible music."

"A small orchestra will be a good hit providing it render some drawing selections each evening. If you should incur some extra expense on account of the music, you can well afford to pay it, as it will prove a good investment. You can draw more people into the church with an orchestra than you can with anything else. The main point is to get the people out, no matter what means is used."

2. "Do not put much stress on preaching."

"Many a revival has been killed just because the minister insisted on preaching salvation each night. This is an old notion and should be put into the background. A modern revival of religion needs but little gospel. We might as well say, the less the better. If there is to be any preaching it ought to be of a mild type, and not the kind that will sound the fire alarm of destruction. How can you expect to do good if you make your hearers nervous? The very class of people whom you are trying to reach are liable to stay away if you will insist on plain preaching."

3. "If possible make the impression that the church is an agreeable place."

"The world has a gloomy idea of the church just because of the manner in which its meetings are conducted. After the people have once started to come to your church, then you must be careful not to introduce anything unpleasant into the services. This is where the ingenuity of a good pastor is manifest. It is his duty to provide pleasant entertainment until the visitors are filled with the idea that the church is a social place, and not a graveyard lot. It is hardly necessary to suggest what kind of meetings should be held in order to please people. If the minister has not yet learned the secret of this art, he is unfit to be the ruling genius over a congregation."

4. "After you have shown the people the agreeableness of the church, then persuade them to join."

"Do not ask them to humiliate themselves before the whole congregation. You ought to be glad if they are willing to join just as they are. It is your work to mould them into a better life by the good influence that you should ever throw around them after they have joined. Accept people in their sinful condition and show them by degrees the advantages of a Christian life, and ere long, they will be filled with a desire to be a Christian. Let me warn you not to be too strict during the first few years of their membership. In all your corrective measures act with great caution."

5. "Do not insist on church vows at first."

"Here is where a great majority of churches make their mistake. They compel a person to stand before the altar and make a lot of binding promises which they can never fulfill. The result of this is very damaging to the beginner. The better way is to take a person into church-membership as quietly as possible, and after he has developed into greater strength, then you can have some kind of a consecration service in which he may make certain obligations. By that time he will not be so much embarrassed."

6. "Never use the altar in revival services."

"You need not take the altar out of the church, you can keep it there for an ornament or for communion service. It will also serve as a foundation on which to place a platform for cantatas and other special services of the church."

"I have given you a few suggestions for conducting an up-to-date revival meeting. And I know of no better advice except to hold no special revival services whatever. According to my honest opinion the best kind of a revival would consist in a special week of prayer, in which each member of the church should pray privately four or five evenings during the week. This method would quicken the religious life of the individual, and would result in much more fruit for righteousness than the usual practice of gathering together continuously evening after evening in the church. This public gathering invites too many temptations that only weaken the life of the church. It is proved to do more harm than good, inasmuch as some of the weak Christians have become discouraged upon seeing the manner in which others are able to take part, and also many become prejudiced against religion altogether by seeing the hypocrites, very often, take a prominent part in the meetings. Also many young people take advantage of such meetings and as a result there is an undue mingling of the sexes."

A Reply to the Sermon by Satan on Revival Meetings

The purpose of Satan is to overthrow the genuine kind of revival meetings, which have been the secret of the great religious movements of the world. The church of God has been revived in every age of the world, and during the special seasons, when the fires of religious zeal were burning, the hearts of the unregenerate have been melted so that they were compelled to yield to the mighty influence of the Holy Spirit. When the church once casts aside the zeal which is born by Holy Ghost inspiration, then it will gradually dry up to nothing and cease to be a power in the world, but we do not fear that such a condition will ever come to the whole church. There will always be a part of the visible church that will honor its Master enough to keep the fires burning on the altar, notwithstanding the low methods used by Satan to extinguish totally the sacred flames.

The several points of advice given by Satan to promote a good revival are only in keeping with his destructive policy. They are all recipes of death, although some truth is shrewdly mixed with his false statements. Satan reveals his meanest trait by wilfully mixing truth and error so as to make the untruth appear like the truth.

Music has its proper place in a revival meeting but when you depend upon that to hold people you cannot do genuine work. If a church is to be a social club then why not advertise it as such, and cease operating under a Holy Cross and a Sacred Banner.

It would be expected that Satan is opposed to much preaching. Anybody ought to be opposed to long profound sermons during a revival meeting, but that does not argue that all preaching should be abandoned just because certain ministers follow in the wrong rut. We pity the revival meeting in which the gospel is not presented. Satan has actually impressed many members of the church with the idea that preaching should be reduced to a minimum during revival services. It may be that some people are getting tired of the gospel and would rather introduce something in its place. There is nothing to take the place of gospel preaching, although many ministers are tiresome, but it is due to their individual weaknesses. The gospel itself is never weak and it can be presented with interest during the whole lifetime of a Christian. We certainly differ from the statement presented by Satan that the preaching should be mild. The preaching should be faithful and fiery; earnest and candid from beginning to end. If it is a fearless exposition of the whole truth, the spirit of God has promised to send it home to the hearts of the people. Human fear and apology in a sermon has the same effect as throwing water on a good fire.

The Devil is very charitable in opening the doors of the church to receive all classes of sinners. He realizes what effect this would have on the church. In a short time the world and the church would be one and no one would know what to call the combination, inasmuch as the church would be lost in the confusion and babble of the masses. If you cannot persuade a man to accept Christ before he joins church, you have but little chance of doing it afterward. Let the church, as much as possible, be separate from the world. Its great purpose ought to be to maintain purity and lift the fallen to a better life. With all the effort that can be put forth the church will still be compelled to carry as much dead timber as it can possibly pull along.

We expect that Satan will continue his deathly sermons until the gospel age will be at an end. No doubt there will always be those who will lend an ear to his black doctrines. But let it be understood, by all who purpose to work for Christ, that the only method by which the world can be reached will be by the lifting up of Christ to the world, whereby he may draw all men unto Him. The special revival services will not lose their power if those who conduct them will hold to the main features of the olden time.

1. An earnest prayer leading up to and during the services.
2. An humble dependence on the Holy Spirit.
3. A consecrated effort on the part of every Christian.

A Tobacco Sermon by Satan

Satan Advances Some Peculiar Arguments on the Use of the Popular Weed.

"There would be no need of discussing the subject of tobacco were it not for those who are trying to class the use of tobacco among the evils of human society. One cannot remain silent when a harmless practice is abused by those who know least about it. Men and women who know the value of the great weed are ever ready to sing its praises. It is amusing to see men or women raise up their arms in horror at an innocent thing like tobacco, while at the same time they wink their eyes at some of the great sins, that are eating away the foundations of home and happiness."

"The narrow-minded critics never look to see the blessings that come to the human family from the use of tobacco. Such people would be surprised if they knew how many millions of people alive to-day would contribute to the erection of a grand monument in honor of any man of whom it could be said that he first gave this innocent weed to the world."

"I want to say for the comfort of all who have learned to appreciate the benefits of tobacco: Do not be alarmed, you will never be robbed of this choice blessing. There will always be enough sensible people in the world to uphold a good thing. If you are numbered with the army of tobacco users, you need not be ashamed of your company. It is not only the largest army but it is composed of the most illustrious sons of the human family, from the honest mechanic to the king on his throne."

"You may wonder how any one could be opposed to a practice so beneficial. Allow me to give you a few of the reasons:

1. "Because tobacco happens to be of a dark instead of a light color. If its color were light like chewing-gum, it would be considered fit for angels to use."

2. "Because it has an unpleasant odor to some. Why should that be an objection? There are many other things that have unpleasant odors that are considered very good. There are some kinds of cheese that are bought on account of their bad smell, and the stronger their odor the more they are worth. There are certain kinds of foods that have unpleasant odors to some people, and yet that does not argue that the food is unfit to eat. The reason why tobacco has an unpleasant odor to some people is because they are dainty in their tastes, or not fully developed in their physical senses. A man or woman of a mature experiences well knows how to appreciate the pleasant odor of tobacco."

3. "It is claimed that the use of tobacco is a filthy habit, but filth is a flexible word. If we were to take a mouthful of our food after it is masticated, it would present anything but a pleasant appearance. We are in the habit of swallowing food after we chew it. Thus it happens that one never sees how much filth enters into his stomach. Certainly much more than should ever reach there. The man who uses tobacco is wise enough not to swallow the rich brown liquid, but to expel it from his body, and because of this wisdom he is charged with being filthy. Would it not be an act of imprudence if a man should swallow all this liquid? I have no apology to make for the man who allows his mouth, his mustache and clothing to be stained with tobacco juice. That is an evidence of a man's untidiness, and why should you place the blame on the tobacco? You mark my word that any person who becomes unclean with tobacco, is also unclean in many of his other habits. Because a person is unclean with a good thing, does not argue that the article itself is unfit for use."

4. "It is further claimed that tobacco is an expensive luxury. This phase of the question is hardly worth considering. Anything valuable costs money, and of all the good things in the world, tobacco is one of the cheapest. A man can get more solid comfort out of one dollar's worth of tobacco than he can

by expending the same amount of money for anything else in the world, even in a lodge or a church."

"There are many other foolish reasons given against the use of tobacco, but it is only a waste of time to consider them. Tobacco has come to stay. It is entrenched forever in the affections of the human race, and it is hardly necessary to produce arguments in favor of it, as it wins its own way. It supplies its own demand and nothing else in the world can take its place. It has cheered many a lonely pilgrim in his journey by day and by night; it has brought comfort to many a heart in trouble; it has sent sweet peace into the bosom of the wretch, when nothing else could drown his care, and it has instilled quietness into weak nerves that would otherwise have become prostrated or shattered."

Not long ago I heard a popular member of the church say that he got more good out of tobacco than out of the prayer meeting. The church and the world would be better if we heard more such words. The best church member is the man who knows how to get the good out of this weed. In his work he is more cool-headed; in his spirit more charitable and in his mind more logical. If I had an option on several men, that would be the kind of a man I would choose to serve me in any cause.

𝕬 𝕵𝖊𝖜 𝕮𝖔𝖒𝖒𝖊𝖓𝖙𝖘 𝖔𝖓 𝖙𝖍𝖊 𝕿𝖔𝖇𝖆𝖈𝖈𝖔 𝕾𝖊𝖗𝖒𝖔𝖓

It is easily known why Satan makes such a strong defense of the tobacco habit. It is his great century stepping stone from the mild use of narcotics to the open door of intemperance. One does not like to be too severe in placing a wholesale condemnation upon every person who uses tobacco. The warfare has not been waged in this direction long enough to open the eyes of all good people. The day is not far distant when the mask will be torn off of the Devil and the use of tobacco will be considered in its true light. No words need be lost to prove that the habit is a filthy one, corrupting both body and soul. The use of tobacco is also weakening. Countless thousands have been wrecked under the terrible blight of this weed, and countless thousands more have had the keenest edge of their nervous powers worn off. One can never tell how much stronger or healthier he might have been in life, had he never been addicted to the use of this weed.

Perhaps the weakest argument used by Satan is the comfort argument, which indeed ought not to be called an argument. It is not a very high type of manhood that must look for comfort in a cigar, a pipe or a plug of tobacco. If tobacco gives comfort it is just because the absence of it would make a person irritable. It satisfies the craving which it creates, and then because the person is satisfied he gives the tobacco the credit of being a comforter. Of what avail is tobacco when great troubles sweep over the soul? At such times we must rely upon the sure help of the Heavenly Comforter, or be left to the suffering of a cold world.

The Devil's Free Lunch Counter

The expense of tobacco is worthy of serious consideration. It is a well-known fact that during a panic when people are starving, that fathers of families will take their last money to buy tobacco rather than bread or clothing for their children. This only proves that tobacco holds a controlling hand over the will of the individual, proving that the use of tobacco so weakens a man that he is unable to exercise his will power as he should. A man should not become a slave to anything in this life, therefore it is better to master the tobacco than to have the tobacco master you.

The Devil's Free Lunch Counter

Of all the lunch counters controlled by Satan none are more shrewdly managed than his free lunch counters at the Theological Seminary. He offers to give free of charge any kind of lunch of which the students wish to partake. He lectures in his peculiar way, telling the students that if they pay the price for Bible and Moral knowledge he will supply anything on the counter free of charge.

Just because one can get these free things so easily the counter is well patronized. There is a dish called Conceit that is relished by the average student. Some eat more than their natural share and consequently become top heavy. The Devil will give anybody as much conceit as he wants for nothing. There is another dish called Doubt which is equally relished by some of the students. Sometimes when the Devil is very busy, he gets some of the Seminary professors to help him in dealing Doubt to the students. Satan is highly pleased to see such distinguished gentlemen working at the free lunch counter. Some have gone so far as to give the students more Doubt than anything else and consequently the student's growth is very unprofitable.

It would be impossible to name all the different kinds of dishes that can be found on this peculiar counter. We find one kind of food is Worldly Ambitions, another is Despair, while others are intended for the lower instincts of man.

Altogether too many give heed to the pleasing words of the Devil who is ever preaching his little sermons behind the counter, and it takes a person of strong purpose who is able to reach beyond the counter to grasp the better things that are hidden. The situation at the present time compels a young man to climb over temptation if he wishes to get anything good. He must reach over the easily accessible dishes containing Pride, Egotism, Hatred, Jealousy and the rest of the immense bill-of-fare provided by Satan to all seekers after truth and righteousness.

We are happy to say that Satan does not control the keys of the closets. These doors will fly open to any earnest mind who is intent upon finding the truth. If Satan had the power he would lock every door that opens to pure knowledge so tightly that neither man nor God could open it.

The free lunch counter loses its attraction to all young men whose aims are lofty and whose purposes and convictions are pure. We are glad to relate that there are throngs of such students at the Theological Seminary who are working to overcome the influence of the free lunch counter. This condition gives hope for the future and promises to put to shame the pessimist who is prophesying that everything is going bad. Where such students are in abundance the Devil is complaining of dull business.

We are strong in our convictions that the coming age will be one in which the present optimist, who rides in his beautiful chariot, will have the opportunity of seeing the fulfillment of his past dreams and the realization of all the blessings long foretold.

How to Keep People from Going to Church

Address Delivered Before a Meeting of Evil Spirits

Once upon a time, the dark spirits in one of their meetings listened to a speech entitled: "How to Keep People From Going to Church." We need not mention how the meeting opened or the preliminary business that was transacted before the subject was considered. Suffice to say that at the appointed hour, a tall, shrewd agent of the Devil stood before a mixed company of evil spirits and delivered the following address:

"It is indeed profitable that we consider such a timely subject. By a mutual exchange of opinions we become richer in our general stock of wisdom, therefore it is good for our cause that we meet in gatherings of this kind. How much we were profited by the very able remarks we heard at our last meeting. Since that time we have been more successful in planting the seeds of Infidelity in the minds of church members."

"If I could hope to do even a tithe as much good for our cause by my present effort, I should feel well repaid for the work it cost to gather these thoughts and suggestions which I am about to give you. In regard to church attendance I would say that we can never expect to gain decided progress so long as there is a large number of church-going persons. If we could persuade people to remain away from the places of worship, it would only be a matter of a few years until the popular craze of church work would be at a very low ebb, and its end would then be in sight."

"Thus I have shown you the importance of this subject before I present the subject itself to you. We have cause to congratulate ourselves on the great success of our work, and if you will give close attention, I will do my little part to throw out some useful hints along the line of my subject. If I were endeavoring to influence a soul against church attendance, I would work along one or more of the following lines, which I will now briefly indicate:

1. Kill the influence of the Minister, if possible.

"This is one of the easiest ways to keep people from religious services. If you can get church members to lose confidence in their preacher, then, even if they should stumble into church, it is not likely that they will get any good from what they hear. When you undertake to kill the minister's influence, you have a right to use any method, whether it is foul or fair. All that you must keep in view is to blacken the preacher's character or get the people to question his ability. If you are a little careful you can easily determine which persons of the congregation will assist you in circulating wild rumors or spreading some damaging falsehood. If you follow along this line with vigor, you will not only gain a point with many of the people, but you may also get the preacher to believe that it is time for him to resign from the ministry."

2. Get them to overwork on Saturday.

"One very effectual way to get people to stay away from church on Sunday is to get them to overwork themselves on Saturday. Persons of ordinary strength can be easily caught in this trick. Urge them to work on Saturday until very late at night, so that when they retire, they are completely exhausted. Then in all likelihood when they arise on Sunday morning, they will have a severe headache, or be under the spell of a languid feeling, that even if they do get to church it will not amount to much."

3. Sunday visiting.

"Encourage Sunday excursions and the entertainment of visitors on Sunday, especially during the time covering church hours."

"I have noticed in my own experience that some good Christian people who are bold enough to go through fire for their God, are easily caught if some smiling friend comes from a distance just before church time and refuses to go along to meeting. Then again, if we can succeed in getting people to entertain company on Sunday, they will naturally go to much extra work and thereby break the Sabbath day, and this is also a good thing for us." At this juncture, one of the listeners interrupted the speaker with the question:

"Do you think it is wrong, Mr. Essayist, even from a Christian standpoint, for one to entertain company on Sunday?"

"According to Christianity it is not wrong of itself, if first of all attention is given to public worship and private devotion."

"But what I wish to know is this: Are we gaining any point if we get a person to stay away from church after he has done all that he could do to persuade the visitors to accompany him. Is it not a case of compulsion on the part of the Christian to remain at home under such circumstances?"

"It appears very much that way, and for that reason I have remarked that it is one of the shrewdest schemes that we can work. A person may not be guilty of sin in each case, but one thing is sure, when he stays at home, that means one more absentee from the church on that day. Even the most sanctified Christian is put to his wit's end, for he does not wish to walk off to church and leave his company at home, nor does he wish to order the company out of the house. It certainly places a person in a trap from which it is hard to escape. Now it is your duty to set the trap as often as you possibly can."

"I see the point," said the questioner, "and I shall make more effort hereafter along this line. It's not hard to put a notion in some worldly minded person to go and visit a Christian on Sunday morning, and then refuse to go along to church with him."

"Ah!" said the essayist with a smile, "you are getting at the point now, and I hope all of you will catch the inspiration of these ideas and work along this line for all you are worth."

4. Weather conditions.

"Make good use of the weather conditions to keep people away from church."

(A) Stormy weather.

"If it should be stormy, you have an easy argument, only be sure to advance it, for it often happens that unless you use your influence some Christians will go to church through any kind of weather. If you are shrewd you can keep many people away from church by suggesting to their minds the dangers of breathing the damp air and the risk that they take of catching cold. If they have no rubbers to cover their shoes, use that as an argument, and if they happen to have rubbers, try and find some fault with them. If there are no holes in them, try and make the owners believe that the rubbers leak somewhere."

"Then perhaps you can make a point with the umbrella argument. If they should happen to have a whole umbrella try and make them believe that it is too windy to carry it, or that it is out of shape. You understand me, bring up anything imaginable, just so you can influence the person to stay away from church. Let me give you a little of my own experience."

"I undertook, not long ago, to persuade a person to remain away from church in London. After I had gone to much trouble to get within hearing distance, I played upon the man's mind, but I found that he was a stubborn case. He was set upon going to church at all hazards. I used a common argument but that had no effect. The rain was falling quite briskly, and finally I suggested to him that his umbrella was not large enough to keep the rain from the lower part of his pantaloons, and, by the way, he had just bought a new pair the day before. This was the opening wedge and I actually won my point."

"This is merely an illustration and it is to teach you how to work one point after another without giving up too easily. You can see that people do not imagine that it is our voice speaking to them. These suggestions from us are not called temptations; they just look upon them as thoughts arising in their minds."

(B) Fair weather.

"If it should be very nice weather, then use your influence to get people to take a walk in the bracing air, during the time they are supposed to be in church. Just tell them quietly that they have been confined enough through the week, and if they should get a little of God's fresh air it would be more sensible than to go into a room filled with people, and breathe the foul air, to say nothing of listening to a long monotonous sermon. In this age of wonderful mechanism, do not neglect to persuade people to use the bicycle or automobile for Sunday riding in fine weather."

"Be bold in your suggestions. A cowardly heart never wins a great scheme. Stick to a person on Sunday morning until you have engaged his mind with one idea after another. Perhaps with a multitude of suggestions you will strike one weak spot in a person's nature, and that will be enough. It pays to work hard to influence a soul to do wrong. We can see the fruits of it in the weakening of the church."

(C) Hot and cold weather.

"If you are a little shrewd, you will have a wonderful help in the extremes of the weather. A person is never so easily overcome with our arguments, as when he has been whipped with the boiling sun until the perspiration flows freely. Hot weather seems to force people into our line and the same is true of cold weather. The opportunities of victory are many, and if you are half in earnest you can keep most people away from church on one pretext or another."

"Let me give you an instance of one of my subordinates. He undertook to keep a woman away from church on a hot summer evening. But no, she was determined to go. So my friend quietly whispered in the secret of her heart: 'Don't you know you are liable to faint on such a hot evening if you are closely packed in a pew and cannot have freedom of motion?'"

"It seems that she had not thought of that before and she had a peculiar feeling right after the suggestion was given. This was enough, and as simple as it was, she stayed at home that evening. There is no fixed law on this point: You must simply learn to make use of the circumstances at hand."

5. Take advantage of social conditions.

"It is true that in each congregation, some people belong to the poorer class. Now you can work a pretty scheme by telling the poor people that they are not wanted in that church, especially because their clothing is sadly out of style. Then go to the rich people and tell them that it is beneath their dignity to go to church where so much poor trash is found. This plan works well in congregations where the society feeling is well developed."

6. Health conditions.

"We must not be asleep in this fast age of scientific advancement. Let us make use of every possible bit of knowledge to advance our cause. Since the discoveries by a man called Pasteur, the people have had their eyes opened to the wonderful world of bacteria and animalculae. You can make a very decided impression on the minds of the cultured people by reminding them of the terrible danger to which they are exposed in a poorly ventilated church, as most churches are. Describe the germs of disease floating around in the air, and in mad glee rushing down the throat, one million at every breath. Be sure to tell them that if there is one consumptive in the church, that they are liable to carry home with them a few million living microscopic animals." A certain evil spirit then ventured a question:

"What should we tell such persons if they should turn upon us and bring up the theatre and other public gatherings of the world?"

"Just tell them that these public halls are ventilated according to science, and that the average church sexton knows nothing about science. The less you argue that point the better. If you get hold of a stubborn case, then try to shift the argument to some other point."

7. Use the arrows of gossip.

"I have known cases where everything else failed to keep persons away from church until they were shot by the arrows of gossip. My essay would be incomplete if I should not consider this point. It is very easy to hire some woman or some man to go to a person and tell him that a certain good Christian in the church passed some insinuating remark against him. Also be sure to let the impression that their going to church is a stumbling block to somebody else. This is a strong point and has been proved to have a sledgehammer effect upon some of the staunchest Christians. You can make certain persons believe that they are suffering for Jesus' sake by remaining at home. If you do succeed in getting them to stay at home, be sure to follow them up, and you may succeed in getting them to stay at home quite a number of Sundays. Then when you have them on slippery paths, you can make them fall with more ease."

8. Stir up controversy whenever possible.

"Stir up a fight whenever you can. Create jealousies and develop a spiteful and revengeful nature. In this manner you can drive out more religion in one day than a person can pray into his heart in a whole week. Now listen to me carefully for some of you do not seem to realize which are the strongest weapons of your warfare. *Work hard to create dissensions,* as it takes very little to get some church members to fight. They will often fight with one another over something worth less than a bone. Afterward some of them will very likely remain away from church altogether."

"When you do get a good fight started, hiss them on. Don't worry about how many feathers are pulled or how fast the hair flies. The more the better. You just stand back and clap your hands and cheer them all you can. It is always more enjoyable to see a set of professing Christians quarrel, than to see a good bulldog fight."

At this point the essayist came to an abrupt ending. The auditors who had cheered enthusiastically during the reading of the essay were also cheering lustily at the last sentence, and as soon as they realized that the essay was finished, they redoubled their cheers. The hosts of Hell will always give applause to anything that is damaging to the church of Christ or any of its members.

Satan on Sensuality

One day we met a man who had listened to many a sermon by Satan on the subject of the lower passions. He had been told that it was good for a man to be like the beast in his body, and in his mind to rise beyond the things that are earthly. This teaching pleased the man, and consequently he tried to develop both sides of his nature so as to be well-balanced. The result was just the same as if you would throw a weight over the wings of a bird and then expect to see it fly away toward the blue of Heaven. The man had been told in one of Satan's sermons that nature called only for that which should be granted, and therefore that he should not deny himself by a constant restraint. It would be a long story if we were to tell what arguments Satan used to persuade this man to live the life of a libertine. He was confused by one fallacy after another, until the finer sense of his moral taste was perverted.

Speaking in general it is sadly true that Satan takes advantage of human inclinations, and strikes his telling blows at the weakest part of man's nature. As a result of this condition we find that there are many willing disciples who gladly render obedience to Satan's black sermons of Sensuality and Adultery. These sermons that seem to have a wizard influence are whispered in the ear of the soul, and blast the flower of purity more than cruel frost would blast a rose.

How sublime is the word of God in its portrayal of human nature. It mentions the flesh as one of the chiefest enemies, and teaches that he who conquers this foe is a real hero, and that he will receive a more glorious reward than kings bestow upon their favorites.

Look at one of the illustrious characters of the New Testament. He forged his way to the front through visible and invisible foes that threatened to overcome him. Paul proved his strength by his steadiness even when the thorn in the flesh was pricking out his patience. He lifts up his praises to God for this bitter means whereby he was enabled to scale mighty heights in his experience. The peculiar type of this conflict brought into exercise the strongest parts of his nature. The power by which he won this victory was the very force that made him master of his times.

If Satan were honest he would confess that since he did not create man, therefore he does not know what is essential to his highest development. But God, who not only formed but sustains the human framework with its conscious soul connected, knows that the pathway to real achievement is rough, and covered with many a thorn. The man who is master of the flesh is a world-conqueror, and some day he will be ruler over an empire more vast than any that earth ever knew.

Satan is not satisfied if a person takes one or two lessons in crime, or if he travel on the soul-deadening path of Sensuality, but he is constantly endeavoring to persuade people to travel on one or another of the degrading by-paths that lead off from Sensuality. One of the most famous of these by-paths is the one called Adultery. Satan or one of his agents is ever standing at the junction of these two roads and putting forth every effort to induce those who have gone into Sensuality to travel off into Adultery.

As you look at the picture you can see how careful Satan is to place the traps of Adultery behind a cliff of rocks, so that they who travel on the path of Sensuality cannot see the destruction into which they are so liable to fall. The temptations of the enemy are manifold to persuade people into this calamity, and if one sets his foot upon the path of Adultery there are always grinning imps enough, as you see in the picture hiding behind the rocks, to pull the trap door, so that he may suddenly stumble into the abyss of ruin.

It should be clearly understood that the Devil is the sole owner of the many paths that lead off from Sensuality. He has one path called Fornication, upon which many are induced to travel. To such he offers a beverage of obscenity which so deadens their sensibility that they stumble on in crime with a thoughtlessness that is appalling.

Another by-path of Sensuality is called Concupiscence, which leads off into a vile park. There are other by-paths to correspond to every shade of sensual sin. Thousands of demons are employed all along this black district, sapping the life-blood of the millions, and destroying the souls of all who allow themselves to become slaves of the lower nature, by following the dictates of fleshy lusts.

We would sound a word of warning: Do not travel on the general path of Sensuality, which is in the territory of the Devil. If you keep off of this path you will not be led into any one of the terrible places such as are indicated in the picture heretofore mentioned.

The only reward that Satan offers to any one who enters upon Adultery is pollution and defilement in sugar-coated form. This, when taken, is so blackening that its stain cannot be erased from the soul by any power except Almighty God, and then only at the earnest supplication of the one defiled.

The Bondage of Sin

A very pious clergyman, while on his way to church one day, met a friend who was under the bondage of sin. The minister was very much interested in the young man's welfare, and he paused upon the highway and spoke to him kindly concerning the terrible consequences of sin. The young man was rich and handsome and, by reason of his standing in society, he had thus far maintained a neat appearance.

The handsome young man did not realize how far he had gone in sin nor to what extent he was bound by dissipation. He was flattered so much by his friends, and he seemed to have such a gay time, that he was led to imagine that he was enjoying the greatest amount of liberty possible.

"Will you accompany me to yonder church?" requested the minister.

One cannot travel the By-Path of Adultery without falling into one or
another of the traps of Satan.

The kind of liberty that some young men are enjoying. "Ah," replied the rich young man, "I will not be held down by a set of church rules. I am bound to be a free man."

"For what reason?" tersely asked the gentleman.

"For your own good and the good of others over whom you may have an influence."

"Would you insinuate that I am not good?"

"I am insinuating nothing. I had only politely asked you to go with me to church."

"Perhaps you think I ought to join church?" interrogated the young man with an air of dignity.

"I am certain that you would be better and happier in time and in eternity if you were to forsake your sins and unite with the church."

"Ah!" replied the rich young man, "I will not be held down by a set of church rules or by the bondage of a Christian life. I am bound to be a free man."

"'Bound down,' my friend, do you not realize that you are already bound a hundred times more than you could ever be bound by any church? Perhaps you do not realize that you are already under a terrible weight of intemperance, but because of your physical strength you are, as yet, bearing it with ease. But mark my words, that burden will crush you to death if you do not shake it off."

"Hold on, parson!" interjected the courteous gentleman, "you are becoming rather personal. If I were a hothead like some men I should reply to you with warmth in my words."

"I hope I have not misjudged you," continued the minister, "I had hoped that you would appreciate the plain words of truth, from one who is ever your true friend. I know I am talking to a gentlemanly man, therefore I pray that you will give heed to my warning this day."

"But why do you speak with such alarm in your words?"

"Just because I can clearly see that you are already under bonds, which if you do not shake off will shackle you to death. Your trouble is not only intemperance, my friend, but if your eyes were open you could readily see what weights you are carrying with you. You are already chained by lust, vanity and other weights."

"Now parson, pardon me for interrupting you a second time. It seems to me that you are rather impolite in referring to me in such a personal manner."

"I am your best friend if you only knew it. By the help of God I would have you realize that you are bound down by something worse than all the church rules in the world."

The young man became irritated so much by the words of the minister that he turned away and ceased to regard his kindly admonitions. The eye of the minister followed him as he proceeded in the course of sin and folly.

If it were not for Uncle Sam, the Saloon Devil would be overthrown more easily. Why does he protect it?

The Saloon Devil and Uncle Sam

Once upon a time the Saloon Devil looked up into the face of Uncle Sam and asked for employment.

"What kind of work do you want?" said Uncle Sam as he bent his tall form to catch the answer of the low Devil.

"To create and satisfy the appetite for strong drink."

"Very well," answered Uncle Sam, "you may go to work at once in any manner you choose."

So the Saloon Devil went to work with a high hand. He sold to the rising generation and those of riper years all manner of intoxicating beverages. The result of his work was very disastrous. He made such things as ruined souls, broken hearts, broken homes and all manner of woe, want, wretchedness and death, to say nothing of the almshouses, asylums and penitentiaries that he helped to fill.

Now it happened that Uncle Sam noticed the nature of the work done by this Saloon Devil, who in turn well knew that Uncle Sam was watching him, but the Devil did not know how to cover his evil work. Sometime afterward the two met again and the following conversation took place:

"You remember, Mr. Saloon Devil, that I gave you permission to do a certain kind of work, but I never dreamed that your work would be so horrible. Now be honest and tell me what you have accomplished."

"I admit," confessed the Saloon Devil, "that my work is looked upon as being disrespectable, and I pray that you will this day make me appear more decent in the eyes of the public. By reason of your great strength and influence you have the power to place upon me a new robe of respectability."

"And how can I do that?" asked Uncle Sam in a friendly manner.

"You can adopt license laws to regulate the liquor business, and by complying with these laws, I can do an honorable business under the sanction and authority of my great Uncle Sam."

"But that will be putting my approval upon it," said Uncle Sam suspiciously.

"You can easily do that with profit to yourself by charging me a nice sum for the license. The money you get through the granting of licenses alone will be more than sufficient to run the public schools, so if there is a little harm done by the business on one side, there will be untold blessings poured out upon your children on the other side."

Uncle Sam chuckled in an odd fashion as this ingenious scheme was unfolded to him. "You are indeed a clever old Devil, and I have a mind to comply with your request. If you pay the amount of money I fix, I will protect you in your business by making it legal. Then if anyone forcibly interferes with you, I will fight him off, even if I must use the whole army and navy of the United States to accomplish it."

The Saloon Devil was highly elated over his fortunate deal. He knew that he could not live long under natural freedom unless he won some kind of public endorsement. He was perfectly willing to pay any price that Uncle Sam might demand, knowing that he could produce a cheaper grade of liquor or sell it at a higher figure, or in some way conduct the business, so that the extra cost of license would fall upon the consumers instead of the saloon-keepers.

A short time after this, one could see the powerful hand of Uncle Sam placed in protection over the Saloon Devil, and the people stood wondering at the situation.

The Saloon Devil, although robed in a respectable garment, continued to do the same horrible and dirty work as before. It seemed that nothing satisfied his greed but the most terrible outrages resulting from the use and abuse of intoxicating drinks.

He always put a screen between the outside and the inside sign of his business. He rejoiced at the thousands of delirium tremens patients that were carried to hospitals, or madly tore their way through the open door of Hell, reeking, foaming and screaming as they went down. The Saloon Devil loved crape, and rejoiced time after time as he saw it hanging from the doors of homes, wherein a son lay dead who had fallen down early under the Juggernaut wheels of Alcohol.

Whenever jails and penitentiaries were too small this same Demon laughed in ghoulish glee, and when fresh idiots were pushed into crowded asylums, he grinned with a satisfaction that was sickening and revolting to contemplate. Whenever a frenzied brain directed a murderer's hand to plunge a fatal knife or discharge a deadly weapon in the Saloon quarrel, this Saloon Devil would cry out as he saw the crimson heart's blood flowing in spurts: "That's my favorite color now, hurrah for blood red."

Such common spectacles as suffering and starving orphans and widows served to whet the appetite of this Demon as seasoning does in the food of mortals. If it ever happened that any one told him to stop his hellish business he would point with pride to his license neatly framed, and declare that he was doing an honorable business under the sanction of Uncle Sam. Just as honorable as the grocery or dry goods business.

No tongue or pen can portray the terribleness of this whole business. By reason of its withering effects, numberless efforts have been made by individuals to check the insolent advance of the Rum Devil. All these proved of but little account. The most effective work has been accomplished by one or another of the organizations having for their sole aim the overthrow of the Rum Devil.

One of the movements that has been, and is still endeavoring to destroy the Saloon Devil, is called Local Option. As this force marches towards the enemy, it finds that Uncle Sam and his soldiers are standing in defense of the whole liquor business. So Local Option, with much difficulty, must labor heavily to operate even on a small area at one time. Local Option would accomplish much more if it were not for the respectability with which uncle Sam has clothed the Saloon Devil.

One day the Saloon Devil noticed the army of W. C. T. U. and he told Uncle Sam that he dreaded that crowd of women about as much as anything else. "They are so sneaking in their work. Their indirect methods and roundabout ways, I fear, will do more to cut off my future supply of customers than anything else."

Uncle Sam looked down upon the Saloon Devil and asked him what he thought of the Prohibition Hosts that were advancing.

"I shudder with dread as I think of them, but so long as I can keep the church blinded to the value of a united move against me, I can smile at the few votes that fall like lead upon me. I have worked harder to keep the saloon question out of politics than you can imagine. I always urge people to pray and talk and wait. Every single vote that hits a saloon, hits me. Bless you, dear Uncle Sam, nothing makes me feel so safe before my enemies as your strong arm raised in protection over me."

"Yes, my son," said Uncle Sam, "and you shall have my strong arm so long as you pay me such large sums of money to carry on your business."

"What think you of the Anti-Saloon League that is arrayed against you?" further asked Uncle Sam.

"I could no more stand before them than I could before any of the other powers if it were not for your blessed hand, my dear Uncle. As long as you place your strong sanction of license authority upon my head, I shall feel safe from the armies that are moving upon me to bring about my destruction."

"As to the church I have but little fear inasmuch as the attack from that source is scattered. I must admit," smilingly continued the Devil, "that if the church forces were united that they could do eternal damage. I am even convinced that they would have the power to pull your hand off of my head."

"Never mind," said Uncle Sam, "just you go ahead creating widows and orphans, filling jails and almshouses, sending thousands to the penitentiary and killing thousands upon thousands every year. Just go ahead and blast the hearts and hopes of many. Continue your robbing, plundering and ruining. I will keep my hand upon your head until there are enough voters in my dominion who shall declare that you should no longer be clothed with respectable authority. Then, my son, I shall leave you to fight your battles alone and not until then."

How many people think that it would be a good thing to take away the hand of protection which covers the saloon and in its place let the verdict of condemnation fall upon it?

Let Us Alone - A Peculiar Sermon by the Devil on Luke 4:34

"These three words in the form of a command were spoken many centuries ago, under strange circumstances. A certain man was filled with a spirit of independence and was controlled by what is called an unclean spirit. This unclean influence was in reality a dignified and powerful spirit who was swaying the man contrary to the wishes of one who was called Christ. Consequently when Christ approached the man He was in the act of displaying His power, when the spirit within the man cried out in commanding tones: 'Let us alone.' This was done in a cool deliberate manner and only because Christ was reaching after territory which was in the possession of another."

"If it were not for the interference on the part of Christ, this world would see what Satan was able to do. It is now as it always has been, if any person has ill luck or chooses to act mean, all the responsibility is placed on the broad shoulders of an innocent Devil. All the black crimes of which men and women are guilty and all the filthy deeds with which they pollute themselves are also made chargeable to the Devil. This unjust condition of affairs has been going on for several thousand years, even before Christ came into the world in person. If the Devil had one chance to prove his innocence and to show to the world what he could do, millions of people would open their eyes in astonishment."

"The so called unclean spirit that controlled the man mentioned in the text is called by all kinds of black names, just because he has incurred the displeasure of the Great Spirit who created all things. Satan works on the same principles that govern the nations of the earth. Whatever he gains by conquest he claims. I need not pause to relate the magnificent conquest through which Satan passed in order to gain possession of this man. One thing is sure, Satan held possession at the time when Christ made his appearance. Therefore, I wish to ask, in the name of fairness, who had the right to this man at the time when these events occurred! The answer is not hard to find. Satan was the indisputable master of that man and no one had a right to interfere with him. Christ took advantage of the situation and happened to meet the man in one of his changeable moods. This explains why he stepped aside from His regular work of the day to win a convert."

"It is stated in the same narrative that the man was thrown around, which will not be denied. Satan did what any soldier would do when attacked. He made an effort to defend his possessions. And had it not been that he was compelled to fight against two, there would have been no question as to the outcome. Satan can always conquer a man when he gets him alone. And he can always keep him under control so long as no one interferes."

"In the light of all these facts the three words of our text are very significant. 'Let us alone' is a fitting command from the mouth of a prince who is well able to manage his own affairs. I will give you a few circumstances under which Satan should be left alone."

1. "Whenever Satan is in full possession of a man or woman he should be left alone so as to complete the work which he has already commenced."

"The reason why there are so many moral wrecks is because Satan is interfered with and nobody else understands how to complete the work which he

At the Approach of Christ the devils held fast to the man and cried out: "Let Us Alone."

has commenced. If Satan is left alone he will bring a soul to its highest development even though it be over a rough path."

2. "Satan should not be disturbed when he is training a person to intemperate habits."

"It is one of the most difficult tasks in the world to train a man properly along the line of intemperance. It often happens that when Satan is about to finish his work that some busybody interferes and spoils the whole job. Some people are very unreasonable in blaming Satan for all the miserable effects of intemperance. Why don't they put the blame on the Creator who implanted such a craving appetite in the individual. The Devil is the most merciful creature living. He takes a man just as he is and tries to give him satisfaction along the line of his appetite, and if the Creator has given him a strong will power the man will be able to carry out the whole program of the Devil and in the end come out a perfect man. Satan cries out to-day in his unmistakable language; 'Let us alone.' We understand our business and no one ought to assume the right to spoil the program which we have made."

3. "Satan should be let alone when he is trying to manage the affairs of civil government."

"It has been of great profit to the world that the Devil was permitted to show what he could do when once he holds the reins of state. The best results that have been seen on the stage of human history have been produced under the guiding hand of the so-called black prince of the air. The only reason for all this is because Satan is a shrewd financier and a safe politician. The most illustrious governments of ancient history were all under the domination of his Satanic majesty. The ruling spirits of the world during the middle ages all drank from the cup of knowledge furnished by the hand of Satan. The great nations that stood between .ancient and modern civilization have been the very forces that made possible the glorious achievement of later centuries. In regard to modern history, no one seems to understand to what an important degree Satan has played his part on the thrones of kingdoms and the legislative halls of republics."

"In the light of this truth is it not painful to see the manner in which some Christians are struggling to interfere with Satan in his own kingdom. Since Satan has done so well in the past why not trust him to the future. We hope that this will be done throughout the world."

4. "Satan should be positively let alone in the heathen countries of the world. Is it not a wonderful creature who is able to bring blessings to humanity by civilization at one place, and at the same time bring blessings through heathendom at other places. Satan has a rightful command over all the dark nations of the earth, and therefore what right has the followers of Christ to interfere? This very interference has cost not only many human lives, but untold pain and suffering to the innocent heathens who are involved.

"These four grand divisions do not comprehend all the instances in which Satan should be let alone. They are merely samples of the situation. And to put the whole matter into a nutshell I would assert that Satan should be let alone at all times inasmuch as he holds an undoubted claim on the world."

Comments on the Above Sermon

Can anybody mix the truth and the untruth so shrewdly as the Devil? Some of his blackest lies are made to look a little white just because he knows how to do it. The foregoing sermon is faulty in construction, faulty in logic and infinitely worse than all that it is as untrue as it can be. "We will make no particular mention of the first part of the sermon but will confine ourselves to the four general reasons which Satan gives to urge that he should be left alone.

1. We do not doubt that Satan would like to be left alone when he gets possession of a soul, for it is on such kind of soil that he can raise the most poisonous weeds if no one opposes his despicable work. He knows very well what the result will be if he can have his own way in any individual soul. He will bring it into full subjection to himself, and will thereby deaden the conscience, blast the virtue until the last fire of hope has died out. Nothing but the blackest ruin lies in the wake of his route and if he were to tell the truth he would unfold a tale of horrors that would be sickening to hear and a thousand times more terrible to experience. It is the business of every good meaning man and woman to interfere as much as possible with the work of the Devil in the human soul.

2. So far as intemperance is concerned it hardly seems necessary that anything need be said. The church or the world is fully conscious of the manner in which Satan trains one in intemperance. By the time he is through with his training he has a body that is bloated, a pocketbook that is empty, a brain that is ruined and a soul that is lost. That is the highest training mark that the Devil ever reaches when he is let alone.

3. In this third sentence Satan uses his most subtle views. He jumbles together one bad assertion after another as if they were all matter of fact. He makes no attempt to prove anything he says, and the great majority of his claims are absolutely false.

Any one who has studied ancient, medieval or modern history is easily convinced that the Devil played no particular part in the upbuilding of the human race. On the other hand he has played the part of holding back the real light from flooding over the countries of the globe, whether it be the real light of civilization or the light of the cross. It was the Devil who inspired the great movement to drown out the hopeful light of civilization in Greece. It was not so much Xerxes at the head of the armies of Asia as it was the Devil. It was the Devil who instigated the movements of the Crescent against the Cross with the endless tales of bloody horror which have not yet ceased. It was the Devil who kept the fires of inquisition burning so as to retard the progress of religious light and liberty. It was the same Devil who ran a race to the shores of America to cultivate the seeds of slavery and infidelity. What more instances are required to show that Satan has had a black hand and a devastating influence over the affairs of men.

4. The logic that Satan uses to prove that he has a right to the heathen countries of the world is about as perfect as a broken window pane. It is sadly true that he has had his own way in many sections of the globe through long centuries of time. But this right of possession does not argue the right of maintenance, especially when the Devil is a liar and a murderer. It is to be expected that Satan will oppose the missionary operation of the church, for he knows that his kingdoms are being shaken more and more as the kingdom of Christ is established. We may all rejoice in the open door of hope through which the advancing columns of Christ's army have entered with more complete victory ever in sight. The Devil need not expect that we will let him alone, neither will our God let him alone for he is a doomed creature. For yet a little while he may show his angel face and his horrid horns, but then he will be confined to penal chains. He will then be left alone with his own and with those who have chosen him for their god, but those who have rejected him will be let alone to work out the glorious miracles of grace in the light of the millennial and the long eternity following.

The Hobby Factory

What we here call the Hobby Factory represents one of the most remarkable branches of Satan's industries. It is a place where hobbies are manufactured for the use of such persons as can be persuaded to ride them. The following is given as an outline of an address delivered by Satan to the managers of this large factory.

"I am glad to meet with you on this occasion. It gives me great pleasure to look into the faces of those who have rendered such excellent service in my kingdom. I have called you together at this time to give you a few additional instructions relative to this particular branch of our work. It is quite evident that the use of Hobbies will never be out of date and in order for us to do more effective work we must improve on our present patterns, and keep adding new designs as rapidly as possible. We have found by past experience that we can reach certain people with a wooden horse quicker than with one of flesh."

"You deserve much praise for the manner in which you have induced many professing Christians to become radical and so narrow in their belief that they can easily confine themselves to riding one of these Hobbies. (Riding one idea to death.) I admit that you have some professing Christians that are hard to handle. They are charitable and do not allow themselves to live between high and narrow walls where the light can reach them at one angle only."

Note: The Devil does not like Christians whose hearts are open to the beams of truth shining from any direction. There is a type of broadmindedness that is well pleasing to Satan but not that kind in which the sincere heart is ever open to conviction.

As Satan continued to speak to the managers he put new earnestness in his voice:

"Whenever you can make a Hobby so attractive that an earnest Christian will confine himself to riding it instead of working in the great vineyard and sacrificing for Christ, you have won a good victory."

"In our work we meet with a certain class of earnest, devoted Christians on whom our teachings have no effect. They are temptation proof and Devil proof. That can we better do with such people than to get them to ride some Hobby. It is my experience that this method proves more effective than any other. If we can succeed in getting a good, well balanced worker to run off on one line until he believes that his Hobby is the best of all, then it may happen that he will look down upon his brother as being his inferior in righteousness, just because he differs from him in opinion. The more we can kill charity among brethren, the more will the power of the church be crippled."

"There are many fault-finding church-members who can be persuaded to ride a Hobby. For these we ought to have some of special design, so that when they ride on them they will be rocked to sleep. When their eyes are once closed to the warfare of a Christian's life, they become an easy prey to any form of temptation that may come along."

"I rejoiced greatly as I looked over the wide field of our operations to see that we have in use several millions of Hobbies. The most of these are special doctrinal Hobbies. It is a pleasing spectacle to behold so many members of the church riding themselves to death on the lifeless horses that have been manufactured right here in this wonderful building. You, my esteemed managers, must not think you are employed in any mean department of my service. If you do your work well, you are entitled to a rich reward. Even the most common branch of my work has its important features. In your labors you cannot be too ingenious, nor can you be too exact. Spare not the staining pot or the paint brush or the finishing materials. Your cares and your pains will find reward in good results. Just a few days ago I noticed that a man of considerable intellectual power, who might have made a good worker in the ranks of our enemies, was switched off on a tangent and it is very likely that the rest of his life will be spent in trying to prove that true baptism consists in being dipped backward into the water, and that any other form is null and void. This is quite a victory for our cause. Not because it is wrong to dip a person backward, but if we can get a person to believe that no other way is right, then he will regard many an earnest Christian as being out of harmony with Bible truths."

Some Notes on the Remarks Made by Satan on the Hobby Factory

It is very difficult to tell what kind of eccentric people the Devil likes the best. There are some people who believe that Satan has nothing to do with making a man extremely radical on some religious doctrine. These same people seem to think that there is no Devil mean enough to trespass on religious territory, and so they have been working side by side with Satan without seeming to know it. A person is excused for holding firmly to any views that he sincerely believes to be right, so long as he is charitable enough to respect another who honestly differs from him.

If a person holds strange views on some doctrine, we ought not to condemn him because of that. But when such a man believes that his opinion or his interpretation of Scripture is absolutely correct, and that everybody else who holds a different view is wrong, then we have a right to believe that he has been tricked by the Devil. It often happens that such a person, in his zeal to push his own idea to the front, will ride his Hobby to death. And when the Hobby falls to pieces the rider usually shares bitterly in the calamity.

Suppose a person is led to believe that Saturday is the Scriptural Sabbath. We must not be too quick in censuring him for holding such a belief, so long as he exercises charity toward those who cannot look at the subject as he claims to see it. Here is a chance for Satan to do mischief by urging a man to violate the first laws of Christianity. We have seen people who held views contrary to long accepted belief, pass judgment upon all Christians who refused to accept their views. Thus they placed themselves in a little class by themselves, and in an indirect manner, gave everybody else, who refused to accept their views, a passport to the place outside of Heaven.

Some of the best people in the world believe in plain dress and surely no objection should be offered against any one for having such convictions. It must be admitted that pride is choking out the life of many professing Christians. The person who rides the Dress Hobby, is the one who is more proud of his plain clothing, than some other persons may be of their gaudy attire. A person can be good and do good without boasting much about it. We have met people in our lifetime who seem to teach by their actions that if others wear clothing similar to theirs it will count to them for righteousness. A person cannot be too earnest in working for the kingdom of God. The more zeal the better. But a person may do service for Satan by holding tenaciously to extreme views on one or more of the complex questions of theology or Christian practice. My friend, get off your Hobby, which does not mean that you must change your faith or belief, but to remember that it is possible for you to be too extreme in your belief.

If we would be like Paul and say "this one thing I do" and let that one thing be the lofty purpose which Paul had, then nobody could offer objection if we pushed ahead with one end in view. If you are in the dark as to what is meant by a Hobby rider, we will inform you that you may know him by the following:

1. He rides in an awkward manner, rocking all over the whole community, making considerable exertion, but scarcely any progress.

2. He wears colored spectacles.

3. He thinks everybody ought to ride the same kind of a Hobby that he does.

4. He has cotton in his ears, and prefers not to hear anybody who tells him to stop.

5. He looks toward the sky because he cares nothing about how many people he may run into, or how many spiritual lives he may wreck.

6. Very likely he expects that some day his Hobby will be recognized as the greatest thing in the world.

Preaching at the Bridge

At a certain place along the pathway of righteousness there is a bridge that crosses a dangerous stream called Temptation. The bridge is substantially built and will carry people safely across the stream, but aside from that it has no special features, as it is plainly constructed, being built for service and not for an ornament. It is well known that difficulty or death will come to any one who falls into the deep, raging torrent, unless he should be rescued by appealing to a power stronger than his own.

Long, long ago, Satan saw the opportunity to ensnare souls at this part of life's pathway, so he built just above the safe bridge several arched bridges of Self-Reliance, each one so narrow that only one person could cross at a time, and even then at a great risk. He well know that pilgrims would not be foolish enough to risk such a hazardous crossing if there were nothing more than the bridges to invite them from the straight path. He overcame this difficulty by placing all manner of attractions around these slippery bridges. At either end of them are beautiful arches of shrubbery, and above them are various kinds of fruit hanging within reach of those who are crossing the bridges. Also the side-path leading over to the bridges is most inviting and beautifully paved, and on either side of it are lawns of surpassing beauty.

It is quite a temptation when travelers come in sight of the plain, old bridge to see leading off to the left such an inviting path and farther away the arched bridges. In addition to this they are likely to hear some well rendered music which Satan is always willing to provide so as to help attract travelers from the way of truth and righteousness.

It is pleasing to know that with all the attractions which Satan has produced, that large numbers are not foolish enough to forsake the safe bridge and take so great a risk. Those who are determined to pursue a straight course are numbered by the millions. The sad part of the drama consists in the yielding on the part of certain travelers. Satan and his agents are continually trying to persuade people to cross the stream on one or another of the slippery bridges, by appealing to their spirit of independence.

There was a young man of strong character who was walking towards the bridge when he was stopped by a familiar voice at the roadside.

"Hold! hold! my young man, why go so rapidly!"

"I am making haste, because I am about my father's business."

"Why not turn in here and see the sights?"

"Because I cannot leave my path," bravely answered the young man.

"It will do you no harm," urged the tempter, "if you turn aside for a while to look upon the wonderful scenery which is close at hand. When you have finished you can cross the stream on one of the arched bridges, and while passing you can eat of the choice fruit overhead. Thus shall your mouth be satisfied, and your heart be made glad."

This temptation came to the young man at an unfortunate time. Ordinarily he would have been strong enough to conquer, but at this time he became an easy prey, and in less time than it takes to relate it, he was seen walking leisurely on the beautiful path toward the slippery bridges, his step keeping time with the Devil's music. After he had tarried a while on this forbidden ground, there was plenty of fiends in disguise who played their part to persuade the young man to cross the stream on one of the dangerous bridges. He was urged to believe that it would be cowardly to go back and cross in the same old regular way. At length he placed his feet on one of the slippery bridges and thinking that his foothold was firm he proceeded with less caution toward the center of the bridge. How could he refrain from reaching forth and plucking some of the luscious fruit that hung above him in such tempting clusters. Quickly as a flash his feet slipped and he would have gone into the stream had it not been for the great strength of his arms. First he clung fast and prayed mightily unto his God for help. Through repentance and faith he was saved, for a great arm of help reached down and rescued him from his perilous position. He cautiously crept to the farther shore and ran to the good old path quite determined that he would try no more to pass over Temptation by depending on his own strength.

It also chanced that a young lady came along the King's Highway and seeing Temptation ahead of her, she resolved to go past it on the safe bridge. She had been warned not to heed the voice of the tempter, so as to depend on a bridge of Self-Reliance. Notwithstanding her good resolution, she was at first attracted by the siren strains of music that came from the Devil's orchestra. As she paused to listen, she presently heard a sweet voice speaking to her. She was somewhat fascinated by the creature who spoke to her so entrancingly that she seemed to forget all of her past warnings. He spoke to her about the glory of Self-Reliance, and tried to persuade her that such a bridge was not only beautiful, but absolutely safe. In one of her thoughtful moments, when her eyes were truly open to the real situation she was emboldened to ask:

"How can you engage in this kind of work? Is it a source of pleasure to entice people toward danger and death?"

The Tempter was not expecting such a question, but he was quickly ready with an answer.

"Ah! it is plainly evident, my young friend, that you have been grossly misinformed. A person of your intelligence ought not to be so easily deceived. We find pleasure in our work, not because it leads people to danger and death but because we are teaching the noble qualities of independence and self-culture. One of these narrow bridges will prove to be a perfect training school to you. Come and prove my words."

"But why should I risk so narrow a passage when the good old bridge promises to carry me over safely!"

"My dear young friend, how can it be that you are so long in grasping the truth. It is plainly evident that the old-fashioned bridge is built for the accommodation of aged people or religious cranks, and a certain few that are so sanctimonious that nothing but the plain old way will suit them. But look at yourself, you are young, sprightly and sure-footed. There is joy in the very experience of crossing such a bridge, and some do it so easily that they can at the same time look upon the rich foliage around and lift their hands to pluck the delicious fruits that hang overhead. In truth, the main reason why so many travel over these bridges, is because this is the most fashionable route. The sweet fruits tickle the palate, and the fragrant flowers give charm to the senses."

After this manner the devilish agents argued for the space of an hour, until the young lady, under the spell of a second blindness, was persuaded to make an attempt at crossing on one of the bridges. She at first placed her foot shyly and when she found that instead of being slippery the bridge was sanded, she ventured with more confidence. Before she was half way across she lifted her eyes and her hands toward the tempting fruits overhead. About this time, her feet having reached one of the treacherous places, slipped and she suddenly fell helplessly into the stream. Her piteous cries rent the air and after a long, terrible struggle she was snatched from the jaws of death by reason of her earnest confession, repentance and faith.

Not all who thus go down are happily rescued. The flood-tide of Temptation has swept and is sweeping large numbers into a terrible death.

It would be a tale too long to relate if one were to report all the deathly sermons preached at this bridge. The most noticeable feature is the persistency with which Satan and his agents plead with a soul in order that he might win a convert for Hell. This indeed is a strong rebuke to the workers of righteousness who often think it too delicate a matter to speak face to face to a person concerning the most important things of life.

All along the King's Highway there are paths leading off to the slippery bridges of Temptation. Some manage to travel over one or more of these places without any visible harm befalling them. This favorable outcome seems

Satan has built three slippery bridges over the Stream of Temptation,
and by an orchestra he hopes to attract travelers toward them from the
King's Highway.

The devil in the sleeping church, or,
The spiritual condition of some congregations.

to open the way for a greater risk and it has always come out true that every person who continues on the border line of Temptation will finally fall to his hurt or his death. There is only one safe way. When you come to the places of Temptation pass over them on the safe bridge of hope, trust and prayer coupled with your good works.

Where the Devil Need Not Preach

There are some places where the Devil need do no more preaching. He has succeeded in getting the souls of the people asleep, so that they are dead as far as real spiritual life is concerned. According to Satan's estimate, such a church is safe only in the hands of preachers who know nothing about experimental religion. If ever the Devil takes it easy, it is when he gets into a church of this kind. But while he rejoices at such a time, he is soon brought to his sober senses when he reflects on the condition of many of the other churches, where he has failed to gain his point.

It is no easy task to put a whole church asleep. The hardest battle begins when the majority of the members are becoming dead. The faithful minority, seeing the trend of affairs, is likely to stir themselves to greater vigilance than ever in the hope of reviving the church to its old-time life and energy. Then comes, in all probability, the great battle. The worldly element, being in the majority, will likely work all manner of schemes to drive out the annoying minority. Many a man has been driven out of the church just because he had too much of the spirit of God in him. It is also true that many a man drives himself out of the church by his own contrary spirit. It is not this class to which we make reference.

It has happened in altogether too many cases that the worldly element has won in the contest, and consequently, the little life that is left is easily choked out. As you study the spiritual status of such a congregation, you will find that the condition is quite similar to that which is pictured in the illustration accompanying this chapter.

Look for a moment at the picture and see how the minister has dropped down into a dead slumber. His spiritual condition is very well suited to his congregation, who are all spiritually dead. Everything else about this church presents an attractive appearance. Both the interior and the exterior are of modern design, and the design is symmetrical. The only dark feature is that which can be seen on the picture. The members of the congregation are void of spiritual life and are dead to that powerful current of spiritual impulse that should fill and thrill every congregation.

One creature above all the rest is thoroughly satisfied with this sad condition. You can see as you scan the picture that Satan occupies a leaning seat near the pulpit, with his feet thrown over the sacred altar, and his head cast backward in the full enjoyment of a good cigar. There is a fiendish smile playing upon his face as he watches the smoke curling above his head, until it touches the ceiling of the large church. You will find a different attitude to Satan if you were to see him in a spiritual congregation. Here he takes no time to smoke cigars, but he is the busiest man in the crowd, ever trying to stir up discord or engender strife among the church people. Satan is powerless when he comes in contact with an earnest Christian, one who is watchful and prayerful every day. Against the weapons of such a man Satan cannot advance, but is compelled to suffer defeat.

What kind of an earthquake would it take to bring a sleeping church back to life! We cannot answer this question. It is a problem too difficult for solution. All we need to say to such a church, after it has turned a deaf ear to all the words of warning, is this: "Sleep on and take thy rest." Or we might address it in the language of that earnest writer: "Awake thou that sleepest." The time will come when those who are not awake will be cast into outer darkness where there will be weeping and gnashing of teeth.

Till All Comes Right

Satan's Song to Encourage Idleness and Indifference

"In life, my friend, as you pass along,
You need not grieve if things go wrong.
Sit down in peace and sing a song
  Till all comes right."

"'You've heard it said,' Go and do your best
Till life's sun sinks into the West,'
'Tis better far to take a rest
  Till all comes right."

"If you are troubled with some belief.
Or feel the pangs of coming grief,
The winds and waves will bring relief
  Till all comes right."

"Instead of climbing a craggy cliff.
Or sailing in some dangerous skiff,
Just lie and breathe with easy sniff
  Till all comes right."

"When things go rough and you're in a squeeze.
Just hold your breath and take your ease.
Doing the very things you please,
  Till all comes right."

"Be not deceived by the toiler's thrift,
Get what you can, as nature's gift,
Let all things take an easy drift
                Till all comes right."

"Rewards all come in the present slice,
Don't look for future Paradise,
Take Heaven now, is my advice.
                And you will be right.

"Throw to the winds all belief in Hell,
Be called a fool, or infidel.
Bury your creeds in an oyster shell,
                Then you are right."

Two Kinds of Riches

A certain young man who was serving the King of Righteousness, was very liberally rewarded with many gems of value. These he prized very highly, and as he went from place to place he exhibited the diamonds and especially the Pearl of great price. He fervently preached to all he met the manner in which he obtained these riches, and many, to their great joy, were influenced to accept the same kind of valuables.

One day the enemy of souls approached the young man, and being disguised, he occasioned no alarm.

"I have heard it said that you are in possession of great riches. Is the report true?"

The young man turned toward the questioner, and innocently told him that the report was true and that even now he was in possession of the precious gems.

"Where did you gain possession of your highly esteemed gifts?" further asked the Evil One, in a manner bordering upon indifference.

"These I obtained from the King of Righteousness, and they are better than all the riches of the world combined," calmly and boldly affirmed the young man.

"What a dupe you are to believe such nonsense. If you take pleasure in seeing things of great worth, let me show you a few specimens just taken from my burglar-proof vault."

At this the Devil laid bare a few shining, but worthless articles, which appeared like gold. "These are of special value," continued the fiend, "and if I could persuade you to make an exchange you would be one of the wealthiest young men in all these regions."

The young man, after a moment's reflection, decided not to accept any of the offered articles. Then the Black Agent told him in earnestness, that if he would make an exchange, he would receive extra a free ticket entitling him to enter a feast of worldly pleasure, adapted especially for a Christian man. The enemy noticed that he had touched the young man's heart, for he was beginning to ask questions.

"If I should decide to accept your generous offer, when would the exchange be made?"

"All you need to do is to empty your possessions upon my table, and at once these valuables will be yours."

The young man reflected for a moment, and then, as if blind, he took the real valuables from his pockets, and threw them upon the table. At once he received in exchange something worse than wood, and as light as feathers. He also accepted the free ticket with a thankful heart.

One night, a short time after this, the young man dreamed, and in his dream he saw a man that looked like himself. He beheld this person as he traveled upon a broad path and noticed that he had the same kind of possessions that had been given to him by the Devil. He fastened his eyes upon the man even until he came to a place where he was asked to place his possessions upon the judgment balance. A moment later a sad verdict was heard: "Thou art weighed in the balances, and art found wanting."

The dream had a wonderful effect on the young man. He gazed upon his worthless possessions and refused to listen any further to the voice of the Tempter, but rather chose to obey the voice of a true friend that sticketh closer than a brother.

"Cast away all your worthless trash," came a voice from some unseen source.

The young man went to prayer, and when he surrendered all he had, the loving Master gave unto him another consignment of imperishable diamonds, in connection with the Pearl of great price. With this endowment he was gloriously happy, and he succeeded in overcoming the wretched enemy who sought time after time to deceive him.

After this same manner Satan is endeavoring to deceive every young man and woman who comes into possession of the true kind of riches. Is it not proper to keep on the lookout for such an enemy lest he should steal upon us unawares in some false garb? Let no one be so foolish as to throw aside the Pearl of great price, and the perfect gems of truth, for the worthless trash that Satan offers in exchange for them.

Satan on Atheism

Preached to a Man who had an Inquiring Mind, but who was Inclined Toward Atheism.

"I am glad to see, my friend, that you are interested in a subject of extraordinary interest. Your inquiring mind naturally looks for evidence before you can believe. You are indeed wiser than the great majority of mankind who accept any belief just because it was endorsed by their forefathers. This accounts for the large number of people in the world who are looking upward to an unseen God. Is it not strange that so large a part of the human family should be so deceived! Therefore I feel the more like congratulating you because of your tendency toward original investigation."

"The God on whom Christians falsely depend is said to be mighty in power and perfect in wisdom, love, mercy and goodness. If God were perfect in love, and power, how could he permit what he does? With these great gifts, he could order everything to his own choosing, and we would not see so much suffering in this world. The very fact that a helpless, innocent child must suffer sometimes untold pain, and a loving mother must endure such endless privations and hardships, are sufficient to prove that love does not rule in the affairs of the world. If love were at the helm, the farmer would not be compelled to contend with all manner of enemies when he is laboring to raise useful products. Every good seed that he puts into the ground is almost sure to be opposed by some insect or parasite that seeks its ruin."

"As you look over the whole field of nature you find that the vegetable creation is cursed by a brood of bugs and worms, too numerous to mention. How could all this be the outgrowth of perfect love? If you love a person your whole aim is to make it as easy and comfortable as possible for him to make a living. The lover does not take pleasure in heaping burdens on his beloved."

"Then look at the long line of catastrophes and wrecks on sea and land, by which thousands of innocent creatures are hurled into a terrible death, without an hour's warning. Surely a person cannot call this the result of perfect love in the world. One of the strangest things about Christianity is that its believers teach that Christ so loved the world that he died to save it, and then at the same time they seem to believe that he so hates the world as to permit all manner of misery and woe to come upon his people."

"No doubt you have often studied the laws that govern the winds and the waves. If a mad cyclone should dash you to pieces, do you think that even then you would be in the hollow of the hand of this imaginary God? It must indeed be a loving God who will hurl a cyclone across the beautiful land of his own making, or destroy the human lives of thousands which he is supposed to love. Ah! my friend, you are indeed too wise to accept such a doctrine. It is better for you to stand alone in your belief, than to be so unreasonable as to accept such views of an unseen Creator."

"If God is perfect in power and wisdom, why does he not extirpate from the ranks of human habitation the horrors of leprosy, burning fevers, and anything else that sends its withering blasts over certain parts of the Earth? One might excuse a person for believing in the necessity of a limited suffering for human beings, but the whole argument comes to an end when you think about the suffering of the brute creation. What has the brute done that he should be punished by privations and sufferings too numerous to mention? How is it possible to account for this suffering in the light of perfect love?"

"You have often looked at the general condition of affairs. No doubt you have seen a chicken hawk descending without mercy and robbing the hen of her beloved offspring, or you have heard about the mink or the weasel, the meanest of all created pests, slyly creeping to a chicken coop at night, and killing a dozen or more useful fowls, all for the mere sake of filling his stomach with their own life blood. A loving God would kill every mink and weasel in the world, as well as paralyze the arm of every base fellow who forces his assault upon some innocent child along the highway."

"Now, my friend, I ask you to meditate on these things which I have presented to your mind. When you have thoroughly digested them, I will see you again and present some of the more advanced arguments to prove that there is no God."

A Reply to Satan's Talk on Atheism

If each person was as thoroughly convinced of the existence of God as Satan, there would be no Atheists in the world. The Devil knows what power it was that cast him out of Heaven, and before whose power he trembles even to-day. The great fact of the existence of God, is the one grinding truth that ever adds misery upon misery to Satan, and which destroys his ambition of ultimately ruling in Heaven and Hell combined.

Satan knows very well the best ways to deceive people, the majority of whom look no further than the mere surface of things, and then jump at conclusions. The Devil takes advantage of this condition and by dishonest reasoning, he leads people into errors of the worst type.

The evidences of God's existence are clear enough to satisfy any reasonable mind, even if there were no Bible. It can be seen from nature alone that a supreme intelligence is ruling over all, and that he possesses the attributes of infinite power and perfect love. Satan falsely argues that if God possesses such power that he would crush out all the evil in the world, which seems to be a fair conclusion to a person who will not or cannot reason. To such a one, permit us to say, that God, in his wisdom, has so arranged things that everybody who serves Him must do so through choice. One of the greatest gifts ever bestowed upon man is his free moral agency, which means his power to do good against the wish of the Devil, or to do evil against the will of God. This tremendous force would be of no value whatever if God would make it impossible for man to sin. What virtue would there be in goodness if a person could not be otherwise. A man would then be like a machine, moving at the will of the operator. Under the present management a man chooses for himself whom he will serve, and we will venture the assertion that one who breaks away from sin, and pushes his way up toward the throne of Heaven, is worth more than a hundred Adams living in the Garden of Eden, providing there were no possibility for them to sin.

When we can once accept the fact of man's free moral agency, then the way is opened to grasp the more mysterious truths concerning the presence of sin in the world. It is through sin that all the pain, misery and wretchedness came into this world. If God had made no provision for man to conquer sin, and its consequences, it might seem as if He were unkind, but since He has made ample provision for us to overcome sin, we are led to see his glory in a brighter light than ever. The highest manifestation of his love is seen as we contemplate the manner in which he bridges the chasm between spiritual life and death.

Concerning accidents, we would say that no man of fair judgment will try to account for each detail of every accident. The reason for this is that we cannot see the end from the beginning nor the beginning from the end. Who knows how many hidden mysteries, how much retribution, or how many new lessons are given to humanity by every shocking accident in the world. It is presumptuous that we who look upon the mere surface, should be shallow enough to criticise the infinite mind who penetrates the ages past, discerns the passing events and foresees the future. Suppose a father is suddenly taken from a large family for whom he has made no provision in advance of his death, we must not be shallow enough to judge the whole event in the little light of the present time. There is a flood-light coming down to us from the past, and a reflex light from the years to come, that give more explanation to the matters of Providence than all else in the world. Things do not happen because God foreknows them, but God foreknows them because they are going to happen, and the reason why they are going to happen is largely found in the mighty will power of man exercised either for good or evil.

Concerning the enemies of the animal creation, such as the mink or the weasel which Satan mentions, it hardly seems necessary that any rebuttal should be offered. The whole family of parasites, from the louse on a child's head, to the weasel, are living and thriving on this globe as the consequence of sin. They all play their part to make man pay the penalty pronounced by God that he must earn his bread by the sweat of his brow. Man who made out of Heaven a Hell by his disobedience in Eden, must learn, by working hard, to make a Heaven out of Hell. Things have been so arranged that it is possible for man to fight his several thousand enemies and yet gain a livelihood, and win for himself an imperishable gift and lay up treasures in Heaven.

If one looks on the other side of the question and sees what unmatched wisdom is displayed in every part of creation, he will see very clearly the evidences of God all around him. Looking at nature through a microscope, we see great wonders confined to small areas, and a perfect adjustment of means to end. Looking at nature through a telescope we see the larger things of creation more plainly, and we are thrilled with sublimity as the great truth dawns upon us that there is no end to created worlds, and that the millions of spheres are hanging upon nothing but the one power which is greater than them all. Each one of these great orbs is moving with an accuracy that wins the highest admiration of man and shows forth the unbounded and unfailing resources of Him who made all things. Here we have before us an endless field of study. Look away from the worlds of space, we find that the human body alone is so wonderful that the most searching scientists or philosophers cannot comprehend the mysteries of this living organism. Such conditions tell us, in mute eloquence, of the great Creator. There are over seven hundred evidences of superior wisdom in the human body alone. It is truly a wonderful, self-oiling, self-appropriating machine which can run for seventy years or more if you throw enough coal into the furnace (food into the stomach) to keep it in power.

So much for the human body; but how vastly superior is the intricate network of the brain. No one has yet offered a satisfactory explanation of the manner in which mind works on matter or matter works on mind. Here is a shoreless ocean on which no Columbus ever embarked.

The Atheist must be blind to the millions of facts that are crowding upon his mind from the world of matter and the world of mind. These point to a force which is superior to Creation, and to admit the existence of such a power is the most reasonable thing that a rational man can do. Atheism and true culture cannot join arms. They are opposites forever, or until the harmony of the spheres can be explained on some other basis than the existence of a supreme intelligence.

It must not be denied that there is a true God whose character is laid open to our view in the book of revelation called the Bible. They who believe and serve Him will some day have the privilege of studying in the greater school beyond this life. But they who reject Him will suffer the consequences of their own folly, and taste the fruit of their own making.

Heaven and Hell

A Short Sermon by Satan Delivered to Graduates of the Theological Seminary.

"Let me give you some twentieth century light on the vital question of Heaven and Hell. You are now in a fit condition to receive advanced truths, for you have finished your seminary training and are able to reason logically. Congratulations to you on your attainments. Nothing is so refreshing as to meet a broadminded man, especially one who expects to work in the capacity of a public teacher.

"You are now able to understand the difference between the figurative and literal language of the Bible, and since you are able to grasp divine truths with more facility, you must be careful that you do not despise the old fathers of the church, who half a century ago earnestly preached their views, even though they hit wide of the mark."

"Let it be said to the credit of the old-time theologians that they preached straight to the point on the subject of Heaven. And indeed when talking on this subject, they had ample material to engage their most talented powers, for Ho preacher could possibly exaggerate the infinite degrees of glory and the unparalleled beauties of Heaven. It seems almost incredible that these same ministers should have gone so far from the truth in their consideration of Hell. Although they have preached some ridiculous views, it is now your duty to correct as far as possible the mistakes of the past centuries, and place this subject in a clear light before the people of the present day. I will give you a few things to remember, so that you can hold to the truth more readily:

1. "Do not deny the existence of Hell, only be careful to tell people that it means the grave, and, in some cases, the word refers to the destruction of the body and soul after death."

2. "Be sure to spare the human mind the harsh conception of fire and brimstone. Tell them that such figures of speech were intended for a more illiterate age. The better way would be to keep silent altogether on such rude passages unless you are questioned concerning them."

3. "Since you are now able to discern between the genuine scriptures and the parts that have a doubtful origin, you can easily throw aside many of the distorting passages, and thus show that the modern views of Hell are Scriptural."

4. "You have also learned that the doctrines of the love of God would require your whole life time to preach, Why spend time in unfolding such blood-curdling tales as the "Rich Man and Lazarus," a story unfit for children and women to read."

Some Things Omitted by Satan

1. Satan forgot to say that the passages of Scripture that refer to punishment in Hell are as clearly stated as the passages that refer to the enjoyments of Heaven. It is therefore impossible to throw aside one class of passages without casting aside the other class.

2. Satan forgot to mention that the old time preaching of the terrors of Hell and the glories of Heaven brought a larger percentage of the people to Christ than the modern, exclusive preaching of God's love.

3. Satan knows that if the opinions of the age do not change that there will be less people fleeing from the wrath to come. Many are comforting themselves by the happy thought that all people will be finally saved except a very few who ultimately refuse all offers of mercy.

Sermons on Preaching

An Essay Delivered to the Devil and his Cabinet by a Theological Specialist in the Employ of the Devil.

"I appreciate very much this opportunity of presenting to you some views and suggestions on the subject of preaching. You are all aware that I have been engaged for a long period in studying and investigating the pulpit work of ministers. Perhaps it is for this reason that I am favored now with the honor of addressing you. I have carefully observed the methods of the most talented clergymen, and I have noted the elements of preaching that are most effective against our work. I shall endeavor to give you the benefit of my long experience, in the hope that you may be inspired to operate along some new and more efficient lines."

'^You will all agree with me that things are drifting in the right direction, but there are still some serious hindrances to our work. These, I am quite sure, we can partly overcome, if we all work unitedly on some general plan, the outlines of which I shall present to you to the best of my ability in eight distinct lines of thought."

"You will agree with me that things are drifting in the right direction, but there are still some serious hindrances to our work. These, I am quite sure, we can partly overcome, if we all work unitedly on some general plan, the outlines of which I shall present to you to the best of my ability in eight distinct lines of thought."

1. "Let us advocate shorter sermons."

"If we keep hammering away at this modern idea we are sure of being well paid for our work. No matter how short a sermon is, we can work to make it still shorter. It is best to urge that a minister of genuine intelligence need not take a half hour or more to express his views on a given subject, since he speaks so often to the same congregation. The smarter he is the less time he will require, and the less intelligent he is the more time he will require. That is the thought that we ought to impress as strongly as possible. If we can succeed in cutting the length of sermons one half, I feel assured that it will be a great victory for us."

"What is the best reason that you can give to a preacher in urging him to preach shorter sermons?" asked one of the cabinet members.

"Besides what I have just given you, I would declare that the people, on an average, are now twice as systematic in their way of thinking, and they prefer good quality in smaller packages. And then I should also say that it is far better to send a few truths home to the heart than to cause confusion by a long, tedious presentation."

2. "There should be as little Scripture as possible quoted in a sermon."

"If this can be accomplished it will certainly be a great hit. Tell a preacher that it is no longer necessary to be reading from the source of authority, inasmuch as it is supposed that the general mass of people are acquainted with the Bible, Just remind the preacher that this is casting reflections on his audience and that he should spend more time in telling them something new, instead of telling them indirectly that they do not know the Bible. If you have the right kind of a preacher just finish by saying: 'Every time you quote Scripture it is like putting sawdust into the gravy.'"

3. "Eliminate as much as possible all reference to Christ in the preaching."

"I admit that this is one of the hardest things that we have to accomplish, and likely it will be impossible to gain this point with a large number of the preachers. But I feel quite certain that we can persuade not a few to put Christ in the background. The best way is to appeal to the preacher's pride, and tell him that if he wishes to be really modern, and up-to-date, he must cut a new swath in the harvest field of the present age. You might as well insist that the old preachers made themselves obnoxious by their constant allusion to Christ. Such references are always painful to the average hearer, as it suggests the dark and tragic scene of Calvary. Tell him that it is his duty to spare his hearers, many of whom have sensitive nerves."

"Allow me to relate a little circumstance that occurred recently. A smart Devil was arguing with a swell preacher, and he told him that years ago when ministers were more limited in their education, they were compelled to make endless references to Christ, so as to fill in the time. 'But now,' continued the Devil, 'some men are smart enough to preach a whole sermon without mentioning Christ.' On this particular point the Devil won, for the minister seemed to think that the less of Christ he put into his sermon, the greater was his knowledge supposed to be. Let me urge you to work this scheme whenever possible."

4. "We should endeavor to stop all preaching about Hell."

"Along this line we have gained remarkable progress during the past fifty years. Our efforts have been fruitful, for we can see all around us that the idea of Hell is out of date. The preacher who still persists in presenting the old-time views on this subject, must be willing to be branded as unwise and illiterate. It would be a thousand times better if we could persuade ministers to preach the doctrine of Purgatory. Then men could sin as much as necessity demands, and after death they would serve their time in Purgatory, after which they would be transported into everlasting Heaven. If you meet a man upon whose mind you can impress the Purgatory views, tell him that all the passages in the Bible relating to future punishment are figurative, and that they bear a meaning entirely different from the literal."

5. "Let us insist en more Science and Philosophy to be interwoven in present-day sermons, as well as the principal current events."

"It is true that some preachers will urge that they were not called to teach Science, etc. But we must insist that preaching is best flavored when it has a seasoning of profane truth. Our victory does not consist in getting a preacher to season his sermons, but that is the beginning, which may result in turning his sermons into pleasing lectures on social economy, or some shades of scientific knowledge. What has been done should be continued on a much larger scale. If we can get a preacher on this incline plane, it is very likely that he will become cold and formal in his pulpit language and manners. If we can persuade the clergy to put more flowers into their scientific bouquets, and more ornaments on the bread plate, we will have but little trouble to make a spiritual feast consist of the most beautiful dishes spread out on an inviting cover, and decorated with modern tinselry. With such board, the Christians will soon starve to a spiritual death."

"It is possible to get a preacher so that he will look upon an error in speech as an unpardonable blunder, and at the same time, be indifferent concerning the salvation of souls. We all admire a preacher who is beautifully exact in his language, and graceful in manners, at the expense of an earnest and conscientious presentation of the truth."

6. "We ought to persuade preachers to get their supplies from below, and thus depend on knowledge more than the Holy Spirit."

"There is not much hope that we can succeed against any preacher, as long as he receives his inspirations from above, or as long as he opens his heart for a Holy Spirit filling, as he calls it. When you meet such a preacher, the best thing to do is to pass on and spend your time on a more hopeful subject. The preacher who depends upon the Holy Spirit, seems to be infused with some kind of fire that is worse than poison to us. I always hate to get near such a preacher, for he sends a chill of terror all over my being."

"Let us do all we can to persuade preachers to draw from the wells of knowledge and depend upon natural acquirements, which, by careful study and training, can be developed to a fine degree."

7. "Push a preacher toward one of the extremes, either Fanaticism or Lifelessness."

"In all this kind of work be judicious. If you cannot get a man to preach in a cold, dead manner, then make an effort to push him to the other extreme, in which he will thunder out at the height of his voice, on matters of secondary importance. Try and get him to talk about Hell excessively, and to picture the worst images that his language can portray. Make out of him a laughing stock as he pounds away with poor reasoning and hysterical appeals. If you can get him at this tangent he will then do as much good for our cause as if he were purposely one of our agents."

8. "We ought to encourage preachers to speculate on the Bible."

"It is one of the easiest traps you can set for the average preacher. Get him to try some text that nobody else ever tried. If you can fill a sermon full of suppositions, it is better than to fill it full of facts. Such a preacher will likely give his congregation more doubt and uncertainty than anything else. There is a particular craving in the human heart to walk on mysterious soil, and if a preacher will make an attempt to solve a deep mystery, he will attract the more enlightened part of his audience away from other things. This kind of preaching will be productive of infidels and atheists, as long as you can keep the preacher away from the heart-stirring parts of the Bible."

"If you cannot succeed with the speculation argument, then try the sensational fad. There are not a few who can be turned off at this angle, and instead of putting a little spice into the sermon they can be persuaded to make it nearly all spice."

A Reply to the Preceding Sermon

It is not hard to see what kind of preaching the Devil would like to have. If a sermon could be cut to ten minutes he would then make an effort to reduce it to five minutes, or stop the mouths of preachers altogether. There is certainly a danger of cutting the length of sermons too short, even though it may please certain audiences. It would be much better if a preacher would put more healthy food into his sermons, so that people would relish a full meal. Some people want short sermons because there is nothing but dry punk in them, and the less dry stuff they eat the better they like it. If a sermon is dead and lifeless, we almost feel like giving the Devil's advice to make it as short as possible.

In regard to quoting Scripture the Devil knows that when a preacher neglects his Bible that he fights like a man who has no weapon, therefore the promise and point of his sermon is gone. Satan has spoiled many sermons by urging that the Bible should be disregarded, and as we look over the field it is sadly true that the Bible is taking the background in too much of the preaching. Some are willing to honor the Bible by choosing a text therefrom, after which a polite good-bye is given.

The Devil says there is too much preaching about Christ and Hell. No doubt there is too much to suit him, but we believe there ought to be much more said on these subjects. Hell is just as real a place as Heaven, and there are millions of people going there. The Bible gives us just as clear a conception of the place of torment as of Heaven, and since it is such a practical subject, it ought to be preached to the people. Not in a tame, doubtful manner, but with a positiveness that carries conviction with it. A proper mingling of the terrors of Hell and the glories of Heaven are necessary to complete the mighty gospel.

No wonder that Satan argues that Science and Philosophy and such kindred topics should be discussed more in the pulpit. If he would have a short sermon and let the Bible out, and leave out Christ and Hell, he would naturally wish to substitute trash. But we pray that the preacher will not be caught in such a net.

It is in keeping with His Satanic Majesty to argue that a preacher should speculate and spend the little time he may have, in considering the mysteries of the Bible, or in impressing doubts as to the possible meaning of certain passages and doctrines. Let us stand aloof from all such foolish suggestions of the Devil. While it may be perfectly proper to admit some so-called speculation into a warm sermon, yet it certainly should not be the ruling principle of a man's preaching. And, as you would shun the intemperate use of speculation, so treat the sensational element. The word Sensationalism is indeed flexible and can be made to cover many things that are not included under it.

The Devil may rejoice over the gain he is making, but the Gospel of the Lord Jesus Christ will be preached by a faithful remnant even to the end of the age. Then at His coming he will gather unto himself the faithful, who shall dwell with him in great glory, and reign with him in the most exalted triumph.

Sermons on Prayer, by Satan and Members of his Cabinet

Satan once met with his cabinet for the special consideration of the subject of prayer. He noticed that the best Christians were faithful in their communion with God and he regarded prayer as one of the necessary conditions to an intense spiritual life. He conceived the idea that if Christians could be persuaded to pray less, or stop praying entirely, that they would soon forget their God altogether.

He met in private interview with his seven chief advisors, and after the session was duly opened he invited suggestions from those present as to the best method of overcoming the prayer habit. The imps admitted that prayer was a mighty weapon in the hand of their enemies, and they were glad for the opportunity of consulting together on such a timely subject.

"I will address you first, suggested Satan, "and you will have the privilege during my remarks of interjecting any question or adding any comments. One of the strongest blows that we can strike at Christians will be to show them some errors in connection with prayer. Let us inform them first of all that it is foolish to tell God anything whatever, inasmuch as he knows more than any one of his creatures. You have all noticed in your experience when a Christian prays, about one-third of his prayer is offered in such a manner as if he were giving information to God. Now if we can succeed in getting Christians to cut out this particular part of prayer we will reduce the time spent in such devotions by one-third. This is a cute little point to work, and while we cannot expect to gain much with every Christian, yet we are sure to reach our point with many of them."

"I would also call your attention to the faith idea that is so strongly entrenched in the hearts of those who send up their petitions to Heaven. You know that it is a common belief that persons must have faith when they pray. It is our work to upset this belief as much as possible and try to make people believe that faith is not at all necessary. You can urge the truth that God knows a thousand times better than any one who prays what is best for the suppliant, and therefore how can it be good for a person to believe in advance that he will get what he asks for. He ought to believe that God will do the best thing for him and leave his own faith altogether out of consideration." At this point one of the imps advanced a question:

"How shall we distinguish between faith and submission?"

The Devil smiled as he proceeded to answer: "Do not try to draw any distinction between faith and submission. If you can tangle up the mind of a Christian with such terms, so much the better. If it is possible destroy the simple idea of faith altogether, or try to make people believe that faith consists in believing that God will do the right thing for his children whether they ask for it or not. If you chance to meet a high-spirited Christian you can tell him that the exercising of faith very often shows presumption on his part, inasmuch as he seems to say by it that he is worthy to receive what he asks for."

As the Devil continued, the seven imps listened with great interest for they were glad to gather some new suggestions that they could use in conjunction with the large corps of workers under them.

"Let me assure you, my friends," continued Satan with an air of confidence, "that one of the most powerful elements of prayer is perseverance. If you are shrewd you can confuse the mind of many a Christian by telling him that perseverance is humiliating, and that in each case where a person asks the second time for the same thing it is an evidence that he had no faith the first time, or that God did not hear the prayer. How could a person have the proper faith the first time and then be compelled to go the second time and ask for the same thing? If you think a moment you will see the confusion into which you can lead a person, especially one who is not well drilled in spiritual prayer. If you can succeed in no other way, then try to appeal to the good taste of the suppliant. Tell him that it destroys his dignity to ask over and over for the same thing and also that it is an insult to God."

The Devil paused a moment and one of the chiefs offered a valuable suggestion concerning prayer in general.

"I have been doing my best work along the line of anti-prayer by trying to influence Christians to copy after somebody else when they pray, or to commit their prayers to memory. I remember of an experience I had with a prominent Christian who was very particular about the language he used in his general conversation. I made it my business to be present with him on a certain occasion when he was offering prayer, and I suggested to his mind that his language was inelegant and that it was grating upon the ears of sensitive Christians, particularly upon those who were educated and refined."

"I was really surprised when I noticed what an effect this temptation had on him. He bought a book of prayers by a prominent clergyman and carefully studied the various ways of addressing the Deity. After this I succeeded in getting him to be anything but natural when he was offering a prayer. I rejoiced as I saw him sailing around in the cold forms of rhetoric, having his mind fixed upon the construction and form of his prayer, more than upon any other feature of it. As I walked away I said inwardly: 'As long as that David continues to wear Saul's armor, he will not do very much effective fighting.'"

"That is a capital hit," advanced the Devil with a grin. "I am glad for the experience that our friend has just given us. I had expected to speak somewhat along that line but his words are sufficient."

Another chief laid his hand on the table and proceeded with the following words: "I may not be as shrewd as some of you but I have won many Christians away from prayer altogether by scattering their thoughts when they were in the act of calling upon God. I have often succeeded in getting a person to think about some of their work or pleasure even while they were uttering words of prayer. The words of prayer died on their lips because their hearts were set upon something else at the same time. In this manner prayer becomes very cold and in a short time the suppliant loses the life thrill that naturally comes to his soul when he puts his heart into his prayer."

"You are a great helper," complimented the Devil. "Any demon who is shrewd enough to catch people in that kind of a trap, is well worthy of high rank in my kingdom."

"I should like to inquire," said one of the other imps who was present, "how you would answer a person who attempts to quote scripture on the subject of prayer." "Just use a common argument and tell him that all such passages are figurative or that they have a hidden meaning. If it happens to be a scholarly minded person with whom you are dealing, quote some sentences from the Greek and that will have a telling effect. If the person is persistent, then make great use of the scene in which Christ is found praying and his disciples ask him to teach them how to pray, and Christ answers them by giving a set form of prayer. Use this argument by itself without reference to any other part of scripture and tell him that he ought to pray nothing else than just what Christ told him. If you can make a person feel satisfied by continually repeating the Lord's prayer, he will be confined to a very narrow channel, and the greater expansion of his soul will not be realized."

These few words in regard to scripture were gladly received by the staff of officers. They admitted that nothing counted so much against them as the teaching of the Bible, and the best way to overcome this was to get people to accept wrong views of the great book and its teachings.

"If we can use scripture," suggested one, "in a shrewd manner we can get a hearing from many a faithful soul who otherwise would give no attention to any of our advances. I remember in a large city I was called by one of my helpers to give some assistance in a very difficult case. A certain person was made to believe that Paul and Silas prayed in the prison at night and that the Lord answered their prayer, and also opened the doors of the prison. One of my servants who had this case in hand tried to show the Christian that prayer never had such an effect, but the Christian was still determined in believing that there was wonderful power in prayer. So I consented to play a part in the case, and I found my subject to be very stubborn. The person in question was determined upon a literal interpretation of the passage. It was then that I told him that earthquakes were very common in Palestine and especially at night and that it was customary to build their jails on a solid foundation, sometimes on an immense bed of rock. For this reason an earthquake would have a terrible effect on the prison wherein Paul and Silas were helplessly confined. It was the earthquake that opened the doors of the prison and if the whole truth were known you would find that Paul and Silas only prayed because they were afraid. After an ingenious twisting of this part of scripture, I succeeded in unsettling the mind of the person very much, but I fear that if he reads that part of scripture a few times again he will forget all I told him. So I have given him in charge of one of my best helpers and the future alone will reveal the outcome."

"There is no doubt," spoke out the Devil with decision, "but that we must be firm on this one point in teaching that there is no power in prayer, and that the only good it does, is to satisfy the mind of the suppliant. Many preachers are taking advantage of the situation and are preaching a good bit about prayer and showing the people what wonderful virtue there is in its practice. We cannot do much as long as this preaching is going on, or as long as we have people who will listen to it. We are thankful to say that some preachers do not say anything about prayer during a whole month. While there are many discouraging features on hand, yet we have reason to be hopeful for a successful outcome if we continue to bend our energies to our tasks and never let go."

"I am glad to note," spoke in a new voice, "that the general drift of pulpit prayer is toward lifelessness and formality."

"Ah! you are right there," chimed in several voices at once. "There was a time," continued the imp, "when fervent and effectual prayer fell from the pulpit much more than in these days, and its effect on the congregation was very noticeable. It is encouraging to relate that we have succeeded somewhat in cooling off the pulpit fire and at this time the zealous prayer is the exception rather than the rule."

"Did not that all come with the advance of learning?" asked the Devil.

"Not altogether," replied a husky voice. "Some of the most learned preachers pray in the most fervent spirit. We have accomplished our work by choking out the spiritual life in the pulpit and the' pew. We are urging preachers and people to move in the rut, and more important than that, to neglect their private devotion altogether."

"I see you have had some experience," spoke the Devil as he followed the words of the speaker with a low grin. "Let me urge you to ply your ingenuity to the utmost in stopping the practice of public or private prayer. We cannot expect to make many great advances as long as there are so many praying Christians. Every effort you make along this line will count and I hope to hear the most favorable reports from you all. Sometime in the future we can assemble and consider this same line of thought and possibly get some additional light."

Satan's Sermon on Jonah

Satan has inspired many utterances concerning the book of Jonah. The following pages contain some of his latest thoughts on this part of the Bible.

"The Bible in general is a good production, although many parts of it do not bear the marks of genuine inspiration, among which is the book of Jonah. This story of Jonah has done more to cripple faith in the Bible than most any other of its uninspired parts, and about the best purpose that it can serve would be to suggest to some good novelist a plot for a good story.

"It may be that such a man as Jonah once lived and that he was commanded to go and preach in the city of Nineveh, and that he disobeyed the command, which resulted in his disfavor and punishment. There will be no harm in believing this part of the story, but when a man of intelligence is asked to believe the fish story in connection with it, then permit us to say that he should be excused from being so gullible.

It is claimed that Jonah, after he had received his orders, boarded a ship for Tarshish instead of going to Nineveh, and that the Lord in his displeasure sent out a great wind storm which tossed the sea so much that the ship which carried Jonah was threatened. All this could happen without violating any of the reasonable laws of nature. But it is further stated that Jonah fell asleep and continued in slumber during the progress of the terrible storm, to say nothing about the great excitement on board. It is rather hard to believe a thing of this kind, especially since Jonah was a Jew. A Jew always looks out for himself, and it would have been more like Jonah to be standing on deck somewhere near a life-boat.

"Then it is also claimed that the mariners cast lots to determine on whose account the fearful tempest was raging. It is claimed that the lot fell upon Jonah. Then follows a full confession on the part of the penitent Jew, after which he requested to be cast into the sea. If this were said of some men we might believe it, but when it is said of a short-sighted Jew the story becomes nearly as hard to swallow as for the fish to swallow Jonah. It would be quite natural for a man like Jonah to work several schemes to shift the responsibility and finally to offer a few apologies. These are the small things about the story that render it hard to believe. But now comes the part of the narrative that no one should be asked to believe. It is said that the mariners 'Took up Jonah and cast him forth into the sea, and the sea ceased from her raging' and that a great fish swallowed Jonah. It is not said whether Jonah went down perpendicularly or horizontally, lengthwise or sidewise."

"Where could you find a fish that could swallow a man, clothing and all? It is a scientific fact that no fish has a throat large enough to swallow a man whole. One begins to wonder what motive the author of such a story had in expecting that people would believe it."

"Not only is the swallowing an impossible task but the story says that 'Jonah was in the belly of the whale three days and three nights.' Anybody that knows anything about fish will testify that no sea-serpent or whale could hold an indigestible lump in his stomach for such a long period without getting seasick enough to throw it out. If this story would be true, one would pity the fish more than Jonah. Think of the great amount of stomach-ache and head-ache that such a fish would be compelled to endure during that terrible period.

"It is a wonder that no one has attempted to write the supposed experiences of Jonah during those three days and three nights while he remained in the belly of the fish. That would make about as interesting a tale of fiction as any author could write. He might proceed to give it in the form of a diary, hour by hour. He might say that Jonah kept awake during the first twelve hours of his strange imprisonment, feeling around against the rubber-like walls and slimy pits of the stomach, until he was convinced that escape was impossible.

"The, writer could then proceed along the line of probability. It would be only natural to suppose that Jonah felt around until he found the hole through which he came into the stomach, and that he pushed his head up through this hole and worked himself half way up toward the mouth and that the fish squeezed him back again. The writer could say, with a reasonable shade of accuracy, that Jonah was so encouraged by this attempt that he made another effort and still another until at last he forced his way up to the mouth of the fish but could not escape. He held on to the great jaws of the fish as long as possible, but at last the fish washed him down with a forced swallow. It would be a happy hit if some talented writer would fill in the whole outline giving us as near as possible the story of Jonah's three days and three nights. Then a person could accept this as simple fiction without being an infidel.

"Going back to the main story it is also alleged that the great fish finally vomited up Jonah upon the dry land. This part of the story would not be as hard to believe as the other part, because one would suppose that the whale would become so tired of Jonah that he preferred to do him a favor so that Jonah in return would never try to get into his belly again. Certainly if a fish could swallow a man, his throat would be large enough to throw him out again.

"Anybody who chooses can believe this story in a literal way. Indeed there are many people who will believe any thing if it is in the Bible, for I heard of a woman who said that she would believe it if it was declared that Jonah had swallowed the whale. But there is a more enlightened class of men who have investigated through many years, and who are very piously inclined. These men accept the book of Jonah as inspired, but in keeping with their good judgment they must get the figurative construction of the whole book and simply count it as showing the bitter fruits of disobedience. But the most enlightened of all the scholars, such who have added to the storehouse of knowledge and have quaffed from the cool springs of wisdom, they do not hesitate to ridicule the whole story and cast it to the winds so far as their own faith is concerned."

Comments on the Preceding Pages

Let each one who reads the Devil's views of the book of Jonah be sure to read the following:

"What the Devil says about Scripture is worthless because he is a liar and a deceiver. It is said in the book of Jonah that 'The Lord had prepared a great fish to swallow up Jonah.' The Devil well knows that the Lord has all power and that he made out of nothing all things that exist, and not only made them but sustains them with a mathematical accuracy so fine that even our most delicately manufactured time pieces must refer to the movements of the ponderous orbs for their standard time. Any man of ordinary sense, just sense enough to keep him out of the asylum, ought to see that a Creator who can make a world large enough to sustain billions of people ought to be able to make a fish large enough to swallow a man."

"The church and the world are getting tired of men who profess to know everything and whose faith cannot rise to the possibility of believing a thing so easy as this. If the story of Jonah is to be turned aside on scientific grounds then many parts of the Old and New Testament must likewise be put aside. But it is a trick of the Devil to destroy faith in any one part of the great book, for he knows that if a professor of Christianity can be persuaded to disbelieve one small part of the Bible, that the way is open to persuade him to discard other parts."

If a man object to the story of Jonah because he claims it is contrary to his reason, he must remember that there is more likelihood of his reason being out of order than that the book of Jonah is defective. Both in nature and revelation there are many things beyond reason, and the important fact is that they were intended by Infinite Wisdom to be so. We can consider ourselves fortunate if we succeed in reaching the knowledge that is put within range of mortal man. The sainted Henry Ward Beecher once said that if God had intended that the Atlantic ocean should be waded by man he would either have made the ocean more shallow or the limbs of man longer. So it is with man's reason. It is not large enough or big enough to wade across the deep oceans of God's truth as it exists in Science and Religion. But we need not tremble, inasmuch as "Underneath are the everlasting arms."

The book of Jonah affords ample instruction to the man who brushes doubt away, but he who environs his vision of faith by a spectrum of doubt will not only cripple his own soul, but will shut from his view the greater glory of God.

"Let us not be caught in a trap. We believe in God and in that belief is included our experiences of the Bible's teaching of his attributes. If we exercise full faith about these small things which are easy to believe, some day we will be transported to a region more vast, where we shall see face to face the fulfilment of tasks a thousand times greater than we ever witnessed in this world. Our present life and its requirements are only stepping stones into the vast temple where we shall see the spring of all power, the center of all good, and the fountain-head of all glory."

Satan's Views on Swearing

Spoken to an Educated Young Man, Whose Conscience was Troubled on Account of his Profanity

"It is impossible to draw the line between swearing and not swearing. There are so many words necessary to give strength to our sentences that he who wishes to be forceful in his speech makes a serious blunder in barring out all manner of by-words. How wisely the good teacher of Palestine said that it was not that which came out of a man that defiled him, but that which went into him. So if the heart is right, one need not worry so much about the words that pass from the mouth."

"The many harmless words used in swearing only add flavor to your conversation and give you an opportunity of expressing the exact shade of your feelings. No one would think of becoming shocked at the common types of profanity if it were not for the prejudice which is quite popular against swearing. When charity once reaches that standard of excellence for which all good people crave, then there will no longer be this deep-seated prejudice against the salt, pepper and spice of our language."

"Constantly remember, my young friend, that you are a free creature, and that you can do as you please. But on account of the civil law try to avoid the rank types of profanity lest some fool should have you arrested."

"Have you ever noticed that the men who swear are usually men of big hearts and kind dispositions. If there is need of charity in the community, three chances to one, the man who swears will be the first one to give substantial help, while the pious church people will possibly not know anything about the needy case until it is too late."

We can see by the foregoing remarks that Satan totally ignores the teaching of the Bible, such as is found in the following passages:

Ex. 20:7, "Thou shalt not take the name of the Lord thy God in vain, for the Lord will not hold him guiltless that taketh his name in vain."

Lev. 19:12, "Ye shall not swear by my name falsely, neither shalt thou profane the name of thy God."

Zech. 5:3, "Every one that sweareth shall be cut off."

Col. 3:8, "Put off all these, blasphemy and filthy communication out of your mouth."

When profanity is so expressly forbidden in the greatest book in the world, and is also contrary to the civil law, then no one ought to listen to the wicked teaching of Satan on this subject.

It is easily understood that if Satan had his own way every mouth would flow with black curses. He knows very well that when a person can be persuaded to take the name of God in vain that he is unfit to worship the same God in spirit and in truth. Or to put the matter more plainly he is lending his influence to the service of Satan.

Satan has a peculiar way of quoting Scripture. He stops short in the middle of a verse or reverses the order of the thought just as he sees proper to carry out his low purpose. When he makes reference to the "Good teacher of Palestine" he quotes the passage in a manner altogether misleading. It is a hundred times better to never look at the Bible than to use it for such purposes.

Satan tells a black falsehood regarding the character of the men who swear. Swearing has never made anybody charitable or kind and it is strange that anybody should tolerate such views. The world has received its greatest blessings from the people who respect and worship God and who could not take His name in vain under any circumstances. The world's march of progress has been along the line of the pure in heart and pure in words. In the language of another let us say that "The man who swears does ten things at once."

1. He breaks the command of God. 2. He violates the law of the land. 3. He transgresses the rules of good manners. 4. He outrages decency. 5. He insults good people. 6. He profanes sacred things. 7. He shows bad bringing up. 8. He dishonors his parents. 9. He does what he is ashamed of. 10. He does what he will regret.

Seven Sermons by Members of the Devil's Cabinet

A few years after the twentieth century had commenced, Satan called a special session of his seven chief helpers. These evil spirits were the highest in rank of all the intelligences in his Satanic kingdom, and they reached their position not through favoritism or partiality, but because of their fitness for it. In terms of our national government these seven devils would constitute Satan's cabinet. In accordance with the call, the select company met and were ready to hear the words of their trusted chief.

I looked upon these famous spirits as they were convening, and although I could not get a close view of their most interesting faces, yet I saw enough of them to impress my mind for life. Each face was a new revelation to me. Oh, how my soul is chilled with horror as memory holds the view! On one face was pictured all the pain and anguish that had been furrowed through centuries of a forced service; another face was such a terrible picture of sadness that no words could possibly give a description of it; and if I had an artist who could draw the third face, I could by an exhibition of it, turn thousands of people from their present evil course to the path of truth and righteousness.

The study of these faces alone is a most valuable work although most revolting. We can see in this life the effect of fifty or sixty years of evil thinking on the faces of certain individuals. How carefully the lines are drawn on such countenances which point as index fingers back to the character of their souls. Human life is so short that the process of evil designs is soon cut off and we can only get the story of sin as marked in one life in less than a century. But think of a demon of great mental energy, who has been biased toward sin, and who has been scheming against righteousness for thousands of years. His face tells the awful story of his past career.

When the cabinet assembled, Satan sat as Chairman of the meeting and his principal purpose for calling the session was soon discovered. He leaned over a peculiar desk and spoke to his chief advisors in slow, distinct tones, with words carefully weighed:

"I have selected seven prizes. The first one is the most handsome, and the rest are graded, each one less valuable than the other down to the seventh. Even the seventh prize is costly and beautiful and will be worn with pride by its owner, but the first prize outdazzles anything that I have yet offered through the centuries. I will not now reveal the nature of these prizes. In due time you will not only see them, but you shall possess them. They will be awarded according to your work during the next six months, as I shall now describe."

"The one of you who will inaugurate the best scheme to help our cause during the coming six months shall receive the first prize. The one who does the next best work will receive second prize, and so on until the seven prizes are awarded."

"When the six months have ended we shall gather in special session and each one of you will give your official report before one thousand judges. When the seven reports are given a vote will be taken and by this vote the distribution of prizes will be determined."

After this plan was fully explained, some less important business was transacted and then the experienced demons went forth to ply their ingenuity against the kingdom of righteousness.

At the end of six months the wonderful gathering convened. The Devil himself was present and on this occasion sat in the center of the audience on a specially prepared throne. The members of the cabinet occupied their seats of honor on a large platform before the assembled host. The one thousand judges were gathered in comfortable array, each one having his appointed place. Beyond the judges sat a numberless host of visiting imps who were also greatly interested in the outcome of the famous contest. At the proper time the first evil spirit arose, and looking down upon the small army of judges addressed them in a dignified manner:

"You are all aware of the special work that I accomplished in the recent past. After a long, careful study of the condition of the church of Christ on earth, I conceived the idea that nothing would help our cause so much as to increase all kinds of hypocrisy (applause) and so, with an army of assistants, I invented certain kinds of machinery for the manufacture of sheepskins of all kinds and all sizes. (Applause.) You all know that it had been customary for our helpers to wear sheepskins during the ages of the past, but as I concluded to carry the scheme into popular use among church members and others, I found that there were not sheep enough killed each year to supply the need. So I have my Sheepskin Factory in full operation as you are all aware. We are now able to furnish any little mean wolf or any large one, with a perfect fit of sheepskin. (Applause.) And I assure you that we have already done a great amount of good for our cause. We are able to make any man or woman appear like a lamb no matter whether his real character is like unto a wolf, a goat or a hyena. You cannot tell our skins from the natural hide. This is the most approved and thoroughly up-to-date method of covering up a person's real condition, and many prominent church members are pleased at the help we have given them to make them look like innocent lambs when in reality they are as mean as hyenas."

"You would be very much surprised if you were to know what a great demand is made upon us by certain politicians and business men. We have made many a guilty man appear innocent and the demands upon us are constantly increasing. (Applause.) Our factory has been enlarged during the last sixty days and we are now running continually. (Applause.) At first we experienced considerable difficulty in giving certain persons a good fit, but I used my best ingenuity to overcome this trouble and now we have a system by which we can give perfect satisfaction in fitting all different shapes." (Applause.)

"I assure you that the sheepskin factory has come to stay, (wild applause,) and its benefit to our cause will be more clearly seen as the years roll by." (Wild and prolonged applause.)

After a few moments the next speaker arose and with his deep voice proved to be very attractive to his auditors:

"What I have endeavored to do for our cause has also been seen by you all. You have expressed your appreciation to me and my helpers at many a place even before this meeting convened. As I looked upon the large number of persons who were influenced by doubt, I conceived the idea that if I could place Sign Boards along the pathway of life and especially at other places where the paths turn to the left, that this would prove very effective in helping souls to go astray." (Applause.)

"At first the work seemed to be small in my eyes, and after I had operated on a limited scale it dawned upon me that I had undertaken a far-reaching and very important task. That will explain why I built a large Sign Board Factory. Then the second thought dawned upon me that these signs ought to be

There are many persons whose black characters are covered by the
Devil's whitewash.

ornamental or have something connected with them to attract attention. I undertook to carry out this idea and that will explain why there is a cluster of buildings around the central factory building." (Applause.)

"You have all seen what beautiful signs are erected along the King's Highway at the place called Downcast Meadow. That one large sign hanging over the byway with the inscription: 'One Mile to Sunnyland,' cost us a great amount of time and patience, but it has already worked wonders for our cause. The colored electric lights 'that rise and fall as they shine each in their turn, is enough to awaken the curiosity of any pilgrim and especially those who may be downcast. Of course, the beautiful colored lights are there only to attract the attention and then the sign is read incidentally. In almost every instance the eye will follow along to the next sign: 'One mile and a half to the Summit of Hope.' Many are turned to the left at this place, and they stumble into one or another of our traps before they realize that 'Sunnyland' or 'Summit of Hope' cannot be found." (Strong applause.)

"This is but a single description. I might consume a long period of time in telling you of the many places where our guide posts have attracted attention, and accomplished their purpose. But the majority of you have already seen all of these, and I am sure that you will agree with me when I affirm that these signs are proving a wonderful help to our comrade spirits when they are trying to lead pilgrims from the way of life." (Applause.)

"The wheels of our factory are humming, and our electrical apparatus is not only up-to-date but ahead-of-date. It is our aim to specialize along this line, and to furnish all kind of freaks and novelties that will arrest the attention of pilgrims en route for Heaven." (Unusual applause.)

The next speaker was greeted with many smiles as he approached the center of the stage. His voice was less eloquent than those of his two predecessors, but his manner was more pleasing because of his inclination to wit.

"For several months past I have been known as the 'Whitewash Devil.' (Laughter.) It may seem funny to you at this time, but I assure you that I had anything but fun when I was studying out the necessary proportion of elements to make my new kind of whitewash, which is far superior to the common whitewash, inasmuch as it sticks better and we claim that it is good for the health. This new Article has become very popular, and to supply the demand we proceeded to the erection of that immense factory with its peculiar machinery. I am glad that we have succeeded thus far in our undertaking. If we can get a Christian to use our goods according to direction he can so cover up a black deed or a black heart that no ordinary storm of persecution will wash the whiteness away." (Great applause.)

The most amusing part of my work is that I have an agent employed in most every congregation who will do whitewashing cheap. (Applause.) He gets the material from our factory and uses it wherever and whenever there is a single demand for it. Even some preachers recommend our improved whitewash." (Furious applause.)

"The whitewashing business may seem like a small thing in your judgment, but I am here to inform you that we manufacture immense quantities of this commodity and the demand is still increasing every week."

At this the speaker walked toward his seat and there was a wonderful demonstration. It seemed that his manner and gestures did more to cause the outburst than anything else.

After the third speaker had finished, he was succeeded by a very tall demon, whose eyes blazed like balls of fire. He appeared to be under a nervous strain and from his appearance one would think that he had enjoyed no rest for several hundred years.

"Let me assure you," he commenced, "that I studied diligently after our special commission of six months ago. My mind seemed to meditate along the line of our equipment for war, and I conceived the idea that our military forces could do much more effective work if we had rapid firing guns that were practical in their operations."

"To complete such a gun I bent myself to the task, and after a period of heavy work I succeeded in perfecting what might be called 'Satan's Gatling Gun.' (Applause.) With the use of this weapon we can make thrice as much havoc in a given time as with the best gun we formerly used. The miniature Gatling gun, which operates on similar principles as the larger gun, can be trained upon a single soul, and it is wonderful how death and confusion can be wrought in a short time. (Applause.) One of my servants who carried a small gun, fired the shots of temptation rapidly into a woman's heart, and she was so thoroughly confused that nothing seemed to be able to counteract the attack." (Prolonged applause.)

"The best feature yet attained is the lightness of the small gun, which enables any imp of Hell to carry it without much trouble. Already there are several millions of these guns in use. (Applause.) We are hoping before long to supply the whole range of the infernal kingdom." (Wild applause.)

The speaker left the stage with a quick step and was immediately followed by one of the brightest members of the cabinet. His very appearance invoked an applause, for it seemed that the whole company of judges were conversant with his work even before he described it. After a moment's pause he spoke in pleasing tones:

"My worthy compeers, I know that my master is deserving of all that I was able or will be able to do for him. After his special commission of six months ago, I aimed to do what I thought would be the greatest service to the whole host of our helpers. As you have all learned before this I compiled and composed what is now commonly known as 'The Master's Recipe Book.'" (Great applause.)

"For doing so small a service I scarcely expected so great a reward as I have already had. All kinds of congratulations are reaching me, and many have expressed their appreciation for the publication of the book."

"Let me read to you a few quotations, which I culled from my pile of letters. My purpose is not to exalt myself but I am hoping that some of these extracts may inspire you to a better use of the book." The first he read was as follows:

"Let me thank you for your valuable work. I found in your book 'How to get to Heaven Without Working.' I never thought of such an ingenious manner of tempting a mortal being, and yours worked like a charm. The book glistens with original ideas, and I am sure that by its help I can do much more work for our master than ever before." (Applause.)

Another letter was rather lengthy, from this he quoted:

"Your book is certainly a capital hit. The last use I made of it was three hours ago. I chanced to be close to an insulted Christian and then your recipe dawned upon me: 'How to treat a person who insults you.' I used your advice with telling effect and I am sure that when I left that man he had less religion in his heart than before. ^'OWST the most novel chapters in the whole book is: 'Fishing.' Not only did I laugh, but I also profited by its timely suggestions." (Applause.)

Another letter contained the following:

"Your book of one thousand recipes is the best literary production in all our kingdom. You deserve unlimited praise for its publication. It seems to me the most wonderful recipe of all the one thousand is the one: 'How to mix Jealousy with Love.' You strike the keynote of the whole question. If we can get a person to try to mix these two qualities we know what will happen to the love part. (Great applause.) Your reasoning in the book is so plausible that I cannot see how a single soul can escape, who gives his attention to the volume. I hope that you will receive your good share of honor for the great service you have thus done for all the forces of Hell."

The speaker opened another letter and was about to read when he lifted his eyes toward the audience and said:

"I feel impressed that I have read enough. ("Go on," and similar cries came from the audience.) I could proceed for a long period of time, but I have concluded to cease reading inasmuch as each of you have access to the book and I assure you that it will never be a secret publication." (Tremendous applause.)

After a short interval the next speaker advanced with a dignity that would be hard to surpass. His voice was well adapted to oratory and his gestures were always pat. He commenced with a moderate intonation and the volume of his voice increased as he proceeded.

"I am not quite so fortunate as my comrades who preceded me. I believe that my labors were just as severe during the past six months, and yet I have been utterly unable to finish my task, although I had hoped to be done before this day. I am building a Medical Factory where the most effective formula will be used in the manufacture of all kinds of chemicals, and also the most perfect apparatus will be used for the injection of these chemicals into the spiritual bodies of our enemies." (Applause.)

"Since I see the great need of thorough work, I am willing to take a smaller prize to-day and complete my task more slowly. So I will say nothing more than to give a little prophecy. I ask your indulgence as I utter these words:

"When my plans are finished you can get any one of the concoctions mentioned in the 'Master's Recipe Book' with a full assurance that you have received the proper mixture of elements. Accuracy in this particular is very essential to do effective work. You are well aware that no recipe would be of any account if improper elements or impure ingredients are used. We are also manufacturing many useful mixtures that are not mentioned in the 'Master's Recipe Book.' (Great applause.) Of all these you will learn more accurately in the near future or just as soon as I am able to finish this work."

The seventh member of the cabinet approached to the front of the stage with a steady step. He seemed to be perfectly calm and his face was set with rigid lines, each one telling its own long tale of demoniacal study.

"Six months ago," he commenced, "after the special commission from our most worthy master, I carefully studied the whole field of our operations and tried to determine where we were most neglectful in our work. It appeared to me that missionary effort was making more advancement against us than any other branch of the enemy's work."

"As I looked out over the field of the Christian church I saw at home and abroad the bright fires of missionary zeal. These fires had a different color from the fires of Hell and to me it was painful to look upon them. How can I quench those fires? I mused to myself. With this end in view I studied diligently and instead of spinning out a whole lot of theories, I commenced to experiment."

"I first constructed a chemical engine. The liquid used was composed of a certain combination of ignorance, selfishness and unbelief. I tried the new machinery in a congregation where the missionary zeal was burning brightly. I threw my specially prepared liquid over the hearts of the people, and believe me or not, I could notice a perceptible decrease in the light of the fire." (Great applause.)

"While the chemical engine was doing its work, I succeeded in getting a number of church members to carry water for me. While they did the carrying, I did the throwing as effectively as possible. By this double effort I am sure that the fires were reduced nearly one-half. (Unusual applause.) Had it not been for some one continually pouring oil from above, I believe that the missionary fire could have been totally extinguished. I know of nothing that can overcome altogether the oil of the Holy Spirit."

"It is my purpose to send imps into every congregation or society where there is the least fire of missionary zeal. And judging from what has already been accomplished, I feel safe in prophesying that we will drown out a large part of the missionary zeal in the church of Christ on earth."

As the speaker was walking to his seat, the demonstration was very boisterous. Some were standing on their feet during the excitement.

The seven addresses were at an end, and as the Devil arose he called for another cheer. This was answered by a deafening roar which continued as long as the Devil smiled in approval. At length he gestured for silence, and the contrast was indeed painful. The ear of each demon was turned toward the stage in order to catch every word that fell from the lips of the great master, who had by this time reached the platform.

"We have listened to seven remarkable addresses," commenced the Devil," The work done by each one of these speakers is worthy of our highest admiration and praise. By inventing and operating new schemes we can only hope to cope with our great adversary, and counteract the vigorous life and policy that is ever manifested in his church. We have learned by our bitter defeats that many of our former methods are no longer of any use. If we hope to win in the great struggle against our foes we must continue in the future to invent new methods for every age and thus be able to meet any new advance that may be made upon us by our enemies."

"But of all these things we will speak later. The interesting feature now at hand is the distribution of the seven prizes."

At this juncture a company of imps carried upon the stage the seven different prizes. The first was a hollow ground crown of gold set with a diamond that had been taken from the Devil's crown. The seventh prize was a golden belt artistically carved with beautiful figures. The other prizes were of various kinds and indeed were a most valuable collection. After the exhibition of these prizes the Devil commanded that the vote of the judges should be lifted. Each judge was told to cast a single vote with one of the seven numbers on it.

When the vote was gathered and counted the result was as follows:

Speaker No. 1 received 107 votes.
"   "   2   "   106   "
"   "   3   "   130   "
"   "   4   "   154   "
"   "   5   "   172   "
"   "   6   "   171   "
"   "   7   "   160   "

After this result was announced each prize was awarded amid the applause of the gathered multitude. After adjournment the army of imps went forth to profit all they possibly could by what they had learned.

Seven great speeches by seven great devils. 1. Sheepskin devil. 2. Sign-board devil. 3. Whitewash devil. 4. Gatling-gun devil. 5. Recipe Book Devil. 6. Medical Factory Devil. 7. Chemical Engine Devil.

At last Satan will be bound in the bottomless pit, whence he can look over the bridgeless gulf to the far-off City of Light.

The Devil's Last Song

The time is coming when this young world of ours will be old and decrepit with age, when the proudest monuments of human glory will have crumbled to dust. The empire of sin shall then fall to pieces and its king shall be chained in the bottomless pit, far off from the gates of Heaven. Can we not imagine that when this time shall have come, Satan will sing his bitter song somewhat after the following lines:

"Long ago I planned in my passing pride.
That to-day I would reign as king.
But where is my kingdom, where is my crown?
Is the bitter song that I sing."

"What joy have I won through my evil designs!
"What peace in my soul-wrecking plan?
I hoped to conquer both Heaven and Hell
But have won nothing more than man."

"I can see above, o'er the bridgeless gulf.
The glorified Heaven-lit strand.
My chains make me feel the double disgrace
As I crouch 'neath the Infinite Hand."

"Where are my princes, my legions of dupes,
And the millions of souls I won?
My pains and my chains are greater by far
Because of the deeds I have done."

"All my plans and my schemes in a thousand ways,
Like bubbles are blown out of sight,
My fancies and hopes like a passing dream
Are covered by shadows of night."

"Come on, all ye dupes, ye millions of men,
Who heeded my wishes like fools.
Take your share for aye of the galling chains.
Under Him who in triumph rules."

"You have lived and died for my noble cause.
Your souls are eternally marred.
You shall see no more than glimpses of light
Of Heaven from which you are barred."

"Then fling all your hopes, my friends, to the winds,
As the echo of sadness replies,
You will feel henceforth the deeper degrees,
Of the Hell which beneath us lies."

www.ingramcontent.com/pod-product-compliance
Lightning Source LLC
Chambersburg PA
CBHW051834040426
42447CB00006B/520